ESSAYS
FROM THE
EDGE

WORK AND CULTURE IN THE 21ST CENTURY

ESSAYS FROM THE EDGE

WORK AND CULTURE IN THE 21ST CENTURY

CONTENT BY

Academy of
Culture Ambassadors
Advocates for workplace team transparency and trust.

CURATED BY GERALD R. WAGNER, PHD

Published

by

Academy of Culture Ambassadors

academycultureambassadors.com

ISBN

978-0-9973708-5-0 (paperback)

978-0-9973708-7-4 (eBook)

Printed in the United States of America

by

Lincoln, Nebraska

CONTENTS

"It's not that pronouns aren't fine, I'm just wondering
if we shouldn't give equal time to anti-nouns."

WHY THIS BOOK?

GERALD R. WAGNER, PHD

These days, there are lots and lots of books, papers, and conferences on the subject of culture. It's a popular topic, for good reason!

Unfortunately, much of what's out there uses boring, repetitive themes like: "Five ways to (fill in the blank)," or "Here's how we (fill in the blank)."

So, here at the Academy of Culture Ambassadors, we thought it was time for something new: a quick, entertaining read that tells it like it really is without the same old jargon.

With that in mind, we asked some of our favorite culture experts if they'd be willing to write an interesting, edgy piece on their topic of choice—one chapter each on something entertaining, readable, and timely.

In total, we invited twenty-five potential authors, and twenty-four said yes! Considering the high caliber of those invited, we're pretty sure this book was a great idea: twenty-four chapters you won't want to stop reading.

And consistent with our belief in transparency, we've included full bios for each author, so you can read about their backgrounds and follow these like-minded leaders in their different endeavors.

You'll recognize that all of these terrific authors are well known in the field of culture and workplace wellbeing.

So, get ready to dive into the best (and most useful!) book you'll read all year! You'll learn, you'll laugh, and we're pretty sure you'll want to pass this on to your friends and colleagues.

Together we're creating a world where workplace culture is as important as a company's bottom line—and the authors in this book are leading the way.

We invite you to get comfortable, turn to the first chapter, and dive in.

Yours in wellbeing,
Gerald R. Wagner, PhD

P.S. If you'd like to author a chapter in the next version of this book, scheduled for 2021, send me a quick excerpt to introduce your content and writing style! You'll find my email address below. All amazing ideas will be considered.

GERALD R. WAGNER, PHD

After graduating from Iowa State University with a PhD, Gerald R. Wagner's career started as a research statistician at a Fortune 50 company in Chicago.[1] Soon after, he became Head of Operations Research/Industrial Engineering[2] at UT Austin. From there he and some of his students started Execucom Systems Corporation, one of Austin's early software success stories, followed by two more software companies in Austin. Then he returned to his home state and the University of Nebraska at Omaha to start up a BSc degree in Information Technology Innovation[3], organize a student internship lab, and to be a senior scientist[4] at the Gallup Organization. From there he went to Bellevue University to start up the Institute for Employee Wellbeing[5] after which he started the Academy of Culture Ambassadors.

1   https://en.wikipedia.org/wiki/JBS_USA
2   http://www.orie.utexas.edu
3   https://bit.ly/35uOhz2
4   https://www.gallup.com/seniorscientists/171815/senior-scientists.aspx
5   https://bit.ly/36w9KJx

✉ | EMAIL:

cultureambassadorsinc@gmail.com

💻 | WEB SITES:

https://academycultureambassadors.com

https://cultureambassadorsretreat.com

🏆 | SPECIALTIES:

- Survey and collaboration software
- Team workshops to arrive at workplace well-being practices for use with the Teams Get It software
- Culture Ideas Exchange—A Retreat
  https://cultureambassadorretreat.com

👤 | AVAILABLE FOR:

Internal workshops for company teams to arrive at their wellbeing practices and implement the Teams Get It software.

HIGH SCHOOL SWEETHEARTS IN "THE BIG STEP"

LET'S GET MARRIED FIRST — 1950
LET'S GET STONED FIRST — 1970
LET'S GET TESTED FIRST — 1990
LET'S DO NATIONAL SERVICE FIRST — 2010

Note: This cartoon provided by the author was not done by Mark Anderson.

GETTING TO THAT MAGICAL GENERATION GROOVE PLACE

WARREN WRIGHT

Boomers don't listen, Millennials are entitled, and Xers are overbearing, soul-crushing parents. Negative generational stereotyping and bias is a real thing.

So how do you blast the bias and get to higher ground—to a generational groove place? It starts with understanding baggage. Yes, baggage.

(This is a metaphor, so stick with me.)

Humans are a bundle of beautiful thoughts, feelings, and emotions, who carry around the totality of their lived experience. You can't separate the person from their experiences—aka their baggage. But since baggage typically carries a negative connotation, let's use a different metaphor: a really nice backpack with lots of pockets and a holder for a water bottle.

Every generation has something a little different in their backpack, depending on age and location in history. So let's peek inside.

DAVE THE BOOMER: MY WAY OR THE HIGHWAY

The Boomers have been around for a while, so they've got *a lot* to carry. As children, they were the pride and joy of their adoring GI generation parents.

Meet Dave. He had a slinky and a pirate map because there were no video games to speak of and no internet. It was a simpler time, an analog world. As Dave became a young adult, he witnessed a cultural revolution. Boomers were change agents, breaking down race and gender barriers.

Transitioning from Hippies to Yuppies, they entered the workforce and went all in. They *invented* the term *workaholic*.

Based on their commitment to their careers and disdain for retiring, you'll never be able to pry Dave's cold, dead hands from the steering wheel of work. It's "My Way or the Highway."

Dave's view is: everything was fine until you came along, thank you very much. You make the world more complicated.

As a gesture, try a two-way mentoring relationship. Ask Boomers for guidance navigating the workplace. In return, teach them the new enterprise software they don't understand. But make sure Dave thinks the whole reverse-mentoring thing is his idea.

GENERATION X JENNIFER: JUST DO IT

I'm a first-wave Xer, so I can relate to Jennifer. Our backpack doesn't have much in it because we're lean, mean machines. We value efficiency, pragmatism, and work-life balance.

Gen X kids were completely unsupervised. On an average summer day in Xer-land, they'd wake up late, pour themselves a bowl of Captain Crunch, watch TV, then leave the house on their bike and not come back until dinner.

Truly free-range kids, Xers learned early to never rely on anyone and trust their own wily instincts.

In the workplace, this survival mentality has made them an extremely versatile, entrepreneurial employee. They're ready for anything.

Best way to manage an Xer? Tell them the goal you want and leave them alone. But also make sure your company has family-friendly policies. Many Xers are doting parents and put their family at the center of their lives, determined *not* to raise their kids free-range.

MILLENNIAL JOSH: FRIEND ME

Sometime in the late eighties/early nineties, people stopped watching evil-child movies like *Children of the Corn* and started watching good kid movies like *Three Men and a Baby*. Popular culture treasured children, and public policy changed course to protect the precious child. Let's call him Josh.

This was the birth of the Millennials, a name coined by demographers Bill Strauss and Neil Howe because of the generation's once-in-a-thousand-year specialness, coming of age during the time of the millennium. Josh grew up in the great recession when both parents lost their jobs, and the pressure to achieve in school was heightened.

At work, Josh values collaboration, is mission-minded, and values the notion of purpose. He makes life, not work, as his priority. He's a super-high achiever, technology-enabled, and wants clear goals.

Want to keep Josh as an employee? Invest in his professional development with skills he can use, maintain a positive work culture, and consider your role as a manager to be more of a coach.

SAMANTHE FROM GEN Z: BE KIND

Samanthe (with an "e," not an "a," because she's part of a generation whose parents are introducing more unique names) is still filling up her backpack, but all indications are that she is smartphone-addicted, highly stressed super-achiever whose parents made sure she didn't fail at anything. This left her highly capable but lacking resilience.

The social media environment of her youth encouraged her to develop and curate her own brand. This is exhausting and contributes to a record-high level of anxiety and stress in her and others of her generation.

But it's not all doom and gloom. The reality is that Samanthe is part of a generation that has the highest level of education; is "woke" to the realities of racism and discrimination; is less likely to drink, smoke, or engage in risky behavior; and might even have greater capacity for emotional intelligence.

She is part of the first generation to have formalized classes in school on SEL (Social and Emotional Learning). Like Josh, you should "coach" more than "manage." Give her a detailed plan with instructions on achieving her goals.

Gen Z wants to collaborate with you to built their plan with milestones, rewards and support along the way. Co-build with Samanthe, and invest in her. She's worth it.

Four backpacks, four different stories. The lesson? Collaboration depends on meeting someone where they are, but you can't do that unless you understand where they've been. So start unpacking.

WARREN WRIGHT

Warren Wright is a leading authority on generations and author of *Second-Wave Millennials: Tapping the Potential of America's Youth.*[1] He is Founder and CEO of Second Wave Learning, whose mission is to prepare the next generation of leaders.

Warren started in radio and television advertising sales, and then in 1997, co-founded Jobfinder.com, which was sold in 2000. He then went on to become Managing Partner at Gallup, where his division provided polling results on Iraqi citizens for the US Army during the Iraq war. In 2011, Warren began a partnership with author and economist Neil Howe, who coined the term *Millennials*. Wright worked with Howe to build two companies—LifeCourse Associates, and Saeculum Research, both using the knowledge of generational theory for research and consulting.

Warren has found his life's purpose in his company Second Wave Learning, where he facilitates workshops for leaders and teams on how generations can collaborate and prepare the next generation of leaders.

---

1   https://amzn.to/2QwLAsS

| LOCATION:
Washington, DC

| EMAIL:
warren@secondwavelearning.com

| WEB SITE:
https://secondwavelearning.com

| AUTHOR OF:
Second-Wave Millennials: Tapping the Potential of America's Youth

| SPECIALTIES:
- Teaching generational theory
- Strategies for multi-generational collaboration
- Performance management and organizational development
- Leadership workshops

| AVAILABLE FOR:
Workshops for multi-generational teams, soft skill training for newly-hired Gen Z, new manager training and development, culture assessment and consulting, keynote speaking, emotional intelligence training, performance management consulting, strategic planning and leadership development.

© MARK ANDERSON, WWW.ANDERTOONS.COM

"Just a smidge higher."

IT'S A HEIST

MATT PEREZ

Running a command and control (C&C) fiat hierarchy is expensive. It robs the bottom line in many ways:

1 | **Expensive managers.**

2 | **Bogged down communications.**

3 | **Power silos.**

4 | **Watered down (dis)information.**

C&C has been around for a long time, and maybe it worked at one time. For many years, it has not. Today, it is slowing down our progress.

EXPENSIVE MANAGERS

Managers get paid more than other employees. They get bigger offices, with more expensive furniture, in the best spots in the building.

All in all, they take a big chunk of the wealth generated by the business. In exchange, they embody the fiat hierarchy. They are the enforcers.

They do other useful things as well, but primarily they act as a conduit for power.

ADDED FRICTION

Communications inside (up-down) and outside (in-out) fiat hierarchical companies are slowed to a crawl due to added friction.

Elon Musk was celebrated for writing a memo to the Tesla workforce.[1] He identifies the problem, but he completely misses the real solution.

He nails the problem: the fiat hierarchy adds too much friction and gets in the way of getting meaningful work done.

The problem with this approach is that, while it serves to enhance the power of the manager, it fails to serve the company.

His "solution" is to threaten managers for doing their jobs.

"Any manager who allows this to happen, let alone encourages it, will soon find themselves working at another company. No kidding."

He never asks, "Why have managers in the first place?" or "What's the value of the fiat hierarchy to Tesla?"

---

1   https://bit.ly/2T0FHpg

POWER SILOS

In another memo, Musk identifies the problem of power silos (*aka* departments).

A major source of issues is poor communication between departments.

Again, his "solution" misses the mark completely.

"The way to solve this is to allow free flow of information between all levels."

It would have been more to the point to question the need for "levels," but that's an easy one to miss today, while fiat hierarchies are normal.

Power silos flood companies with misinformation. "Super dumb things" happen, but they are a necessary side-effect of the fiat hierarchy.

If, in order to get something done between departments, an individual contributor has to talk to their manager, who talks to a director, who talks to a VP, who talks to another VP, who talks to a director, who talks to a manager, who talks to someone doing the actual work, then super dumb things will happen.

At the end of the paragraph, Musk pleads:

"It must be okay for people to talk directly and just make the right thing happen."

Yes, it is okay for people to talk to one another directly. And it's faster. And less expensive. And more innovative. And more meaningful and satisfying for everyone involved.

The *only* thing it requires is for everyone to lead with trust and to treat each other as adults. Simple.

MATT PEREZ

Matt has been building hardware and software products for over thirty years. He has helped raise close to $50M in VC investments as a co-founder of three startups.

He co-founded Nearsoft, Inc, a successful software development company that helps its clients grow their software development teams with engineers in Mexico.

After working in traditional hierarchical, fear-driven organizations for many years, Matt got a chance to experiment with organizational freedom and co-management at Nearsoft. The experiment is going well, and Nearsoft is very successful, thanks to its culture.

◍ | LOCATION:

San Jose, California

✉ | EMAIL:

mperez@nearsoft.com

🖵 | WEB SITE:

https://nearsoft.com/contact

🏆 | SPECIALTIES:

- Co-management, from twelve years of experience at Nearsoft
- Co-ownership, from the experience of what we *didn't do* at Nearsoft and what I've researched since
- Pros and cons of packaged solutions, like Holacracy
- Strategy for moving away from fiat hierarchy

"Damn webcam! Now *everyone* knows
I'm a dog!"

A BEAUTIFUL PARADOX (AND WHY ANONYMITY SHOULD BE ABOLISHED IN THE WORKPLACE)

NANCI MEADOWS

For a few years our company has employed an awesome team member engagement software tool. It does all the things such a tool should: encourage responses to mini-surveys, garner feedback, and even allow for peer-to-peer recognition in fun and playful ways.

Team members love it and are absolutely more engaged because of it.

But I'm beginning to *hate* it. In fact, I suspect it may be causing permanent damage to our team members and, consequently, to our whole company.

You see, our corporate philosophy is one of freedom, collaboration, and personal responsibility. Our primary core tenet is that "people do not manage people; people manage commitments." Our core value of authenticity is based on the idea that we can be our true, genuine selves in a safe environment.

In keeping with these beliefs, we encourage direct and difficult conversations. We openly declare that we do not have "issue escalation" in our organization; we have "issue resolution."

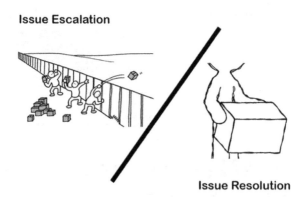

Issue Escalation

Issue Resolution

ISSUE ESCALATION VS. ISSUE RESOLUTION

In many traditionally hierarchical organizations, people will take their issues to a designated individual and "lob them over the fence." They walk away glad to be rid of the issue and are hopeful that the appropriate person gets it resolved.

In our environment of self-management, we employ issue resolution instead. We readily recognize that there is no one on the other side of that fence. In fact, we are all on the same side—if you have an issue, it's just that: yours.

As a team, we provide collaborative support and understanding when individuals need to manage an issue. We develop processes and tools that make it easier for us to address and resolve our own challenges together.

(For sensitive issues like harassment or discrimination, of course confidentiality is in order. We would never expect anyone to have to resolve that sort of issue on their own. But confidentiality is not anonymity, and the distinction is an important one.)

ANONYMITY REMOVES ACCOUNTABILITY

Where I've begun to struggle with our engagement tool is in the anonymity it encourages. In the tool, team members can add anonymous suggestions coworkers are able to see. Sometimes these submissions are downright unkind.

Once a colleague brought his well-behaved nine-year-old son into the office, and within five minutes someone anonymously "suggested" that people should give warning when they're bringing children, so others can stay home if they want. Ouch!

Would this have been said out loud by anyone, ever? Not a chance! But allow for anonymity, and the barriers of decency and kindness are somehow too easily breached.

By providing an avenue for people to "lob comments over the fence," we've effectively violated our own belief system. But even more concerning is the damage we're inflicting on our team members who are sending those comments. Here's how.

We believe that direct communication, transparency, and full disclosure are all elements of a strong, healthy, and vibrant community. But we all know that difficult conversations are just that—difficult! I mean, how do you tell a colleague that you struggle when their child is in the office? The key is collective awareness and open acknowledgment.

It's important to recognize that our strength lies in our complete and utter vulnerability. This is a beautiful paradox.

Here's an example. Kintsugi is a lovely ancient Japanese practice where broken pottery is mended using a special lacquer dusted with gold, silver, or platinum. This method gives the repaired piece an entirely new look that does not hide the damage but *highlights* it.

The cracks on the ceramic bowl do not represent the end of its useful life, but rather call attention to what *was* once its weakness. The declared brokenness now becomes the object's greatest strength. The piece is clearly more beautiful for having been flawed.

Anonymity is the opposite of such vulnerability.

ANONYMITY FINDS ITS ORIGINS IN FEAR

An anonymous comment once came through our engagement tool that called our office administrator's efforts to supply our kitchen with desirable snacks "a joke." Our office administrator was understandably disappointed, but because the hurtful comment came anonymously, they immediately felt unsafe among their own team.

Who was it that made that comment? It could be anyone—or everyone! What if everyone has been talking about it together, and only one of them was "brave" enough to put it into words? So the internal voice of fear begins its relentless rampage until this person who had been quite happy and confident is now hurt and afraid to act.

We empathize with our office administrator in this example, but what of the person who made the anonymous comment? I contend that they are also a casualty of this scenario.

When we are fearful of not only sharing but of *owning* our thoughts or words, we are losing out on freedom, growth, and acceptance. Hiding behind anonymity may mean "safety" in the immediate but ultimately results in isolation and uncertainty.

Those who learn how to be open-hearted and courageous in their relationships, saying difficult words out loud, and acknowledging their weaknesses or fears are the ones who ultimately are freed from those same fears.

Yes, their brokenness is out there for all the world to see, but they are not shamed for the damage they reveal. On the contrary, in the same way that the gilded bowl is valued for its revelation, the one who reveals their vulnerability is appreciated and granted understanding.

As founders and leaders of organizations in which our colleagues spend their working lives, we must cultivate environments that stimulate genuine openness. Cultures of transparent communication will inspire personal commitments to authenticity, respect, and kindness in the safety of mutual dependence.

Ask yourself, who among us would not love to live in that fearless world?

NANCI MEADOWS

Nanci Meadows is the People Champion of Hubb, an event management software company in Vancouver, WA. The awesome team at Hubb builds products that power some of the largest events in the world, including HubSpot and Microsoft Ignite.

Having worked with teams in the areas of process improvement and execution excellence for over twenty years, Nanci's primary focus has evolved into creating cultures where every team member is able to be the full, wonderful, amazing adult at work as they are anywhere else in life. Hubb colleagues agree, "there is no such thing as work-life balance—there's just this one life, and you happen to be living some of it here." This near-nirvana is achieved through a self-managed teams methodology. When people are free to manage their commitments (not each other) exciting and innovative things begin to happen!

Nanci was the 2016 Portland Business Journal HR Leadership Award winner for her efforts in liberating teams to achieve their highest potential through self-management.

◎ | LOCATION:

Vancouver, Washington

✉ | EMAIL:

nmeadows@hubb.me

💻 | WEB SITE:

https://hubb.me

🏆 | SPECIALTIES:

- Self-managed teams
- Compensation as culture

👤 | AVAILABLE FOR:

Conference speaking, self-managed teams consultation, and coffee, anytime, so long as the topic is
freedom in the workplace.

"Who's the new guy?"

LOUSY ONBOARDING IS EXPENSIVE

CHRIS M. MURCHISON

A colleague once shared a story of a vice president they worked with who was courted and eventually lured away by a competitor. It was a clear win for the competing organization.

However, when she showed up on her first day, she was taken to her new office where she sat alone for several hours. Her manager was traveling, and her new colleagues weren't even aware of her arrival.

It was a bad beginning and didn't get much better. She left after only three months on the job. That initial win turned into a loss for the new company.

SINK OR SWIM?

I wish this were a rare story, but sadly, the stories I hear indicate that many companies are so eager for employees to hit the ground running that they neglect meaningful onboarding. New hires are quickly dropped into the deep end and expected to learn to swim ASAP. This plunge can be a thrilling challenge for some, but many find it stressful. In fact, the anxiety and lack of onboarding support can drive 17 percent of new hires to leave their jobs within three months[1] of their start date.

The fiscal impact of such early attrition is significant; between 100 percent and 300 percent of the employee's salary, a poor return on investment.

The human cost of poor onboarding is also significant. Low confidence, impostor syndrome,[2] and a lack of belonging are common consequences, resulting in decreased productivity, creativity, and commitment.

A BETTER BEGINNING

Employees deserve better. A well-planned onboarding experience brings out the best in new hires, reinforces an organization's purpose and values, and enacts important cultural practices and rituals. Win, win, win!

Research[3] shows that thoughtful onboarding programs lead to higher ROI:

- New employees who go through structured onboarding program are 58 percent more likely to be with the organization after three years.

- Organizations with a standard onboarding process experience 50 percent greater new hire productivity.

- Manager satisfaction increases by 20 percent when direct reports have formal onboarding training.

---

1   https://www.shrm.org/resourcesandtools/hr-topics/talent-acquisition/pages/onboard ing-key-retaining-engaging-talent.aspx

2   https://time.com/5312483/how-to-deal-with-impostor-syndrome/

3   http://blog.clickboarding.com/18-jaw-dropping-onboarding-stats-you-need-to-know

WHAT TO DO?

Rapid growth, busyness, and lack of funding are poor excuses for not paying attention to this important process. What can organizations do right now to elevate their onboarding practices? Rethink the purpose and meaning of onboarding and experiment with some new approaches to transform the experience.

1 | Remember, there's only <u>one</u> first day.

My former boss and friend, Pat Christen,[4] once said, "As humans, we give disproportionate weight to what happens to us at the start of relationships. If you pay a lot of attention to those early days of engagement, you get a lot of leverage and mileage out of the way people end up feeling about themselves and about the environment that they are working in … A first impression is a lasting and impactful one."

Try this: Be an exceptional host and make the first day positively memorable. Within the first few weeks, ask new employees how the expectations they had match up against their actual experience in the organization. If there's misalignment, leverage that as an opportunity to rethink your onboarding strategy.

2 | Focus more on the employee than the organization.

The default assumption for most onboarding programs is that they must orient new hires to the organization's identity, mission and values, history, structure and strategy, and more. Leaders and department heads are marched in, and new hires sit through presentations, sometimes for hours on end, which constitutes one-way communication.

Research[5] conducted with an organization called WyPro showed that when a new hire's identity is emphasized over the organization's, employee engagement and retention increased by 250 percent.

Try this: Identify a place in your onboarding process where you can help new hires reflect on this career transition. What excites them about

---

4   https://www.youtube.com/watch?v=UJuoXe4K0sU&feature=youtu.be
5   https://bit.ly/35wqVJo

this new opportunity? What challenges do they anticipate? What do they hope to learn and contribute? Who do they want to become? This could be achieved through an assessment tool, reflective exercises, generative conversations with their new manager or an assigned buddy or mentor, and more.

3 | Leverage connection; build belonging.

Set your new hires up for success by meaningfully connecting them to their manager, their new team and others they will work with. These connections should be made immediately, particularly with the new employee's manager. If the manager cannot be onsite, delay the start date!

Try this: Introduce new hires to colleagues who might share similar hobbies or backgrounds, people who might become new friends. Doing this welcomes the individual to your organization and supports engagement and belonging.

ONBOARDING PAYS OFF

Your onboarding practice is a microcosm of your organization's culture. How you treat new team members signals what is important. Are you sending the message you want? Pay attention to your beginnings, and you'll reap the rewards.

CHRIS M. MURCHISON

Chris is a passionate advocate for positive workplace culture. In his broad career spanning the higher education, for-profit, not-for-profit, and foundation sectors, he has focused his energy on developing creative means to build community in the workplace.

In 2014, Chris was named the first Visiting Leader at the Center for Positive Organizations in the University of Michigan's Ross School of Business. In 2018, Chris was additionally appointed to the Advisory Board of the International Positive Psychology Association's Work & Organizations Division.

Chris currently works as a creative thought partner, consultant, and coach to organizations ready to reimagine their cultures.

⊕ | LOCATION:
San Francisco, California

✉ | EMAIL:
chris.murchison@gmail.com

🖥 | WEB SITE:
https://linkedin.com/pulse/elevate-your-onboard-ing-better-engagement-chris-marcell-murchison

🏆 | SPECIALTIES:
- Organization beginnings and endings (onboardings and transitions out of organizations)
- Experience design
- Group conversation facilitation
- Applied improvisation
- Connective activity design and facilitation
- Emotional intelligence training
- Diversity, equity and inclusion training
- Strengthscope certified coach
- MBTI certified

👤 | AVAILABLE FOR:
Organization culture consultation, creative thought partnership, retreat design and facilitation, course design, and keynote speaking.

"I unleashed my creativity, but it ran away."

CREATIVITY DOESN'T JUST HAPPEN

MARIA GATLING

For many of us, creativity, or "to be creative," is somewhat of a mystery. We understand the concept about as much as we understand most artists.

According to the dictionary, creativity is the use of the imagination or the creation of original ideas, especially in the production of an artistic work. That's great, but we still don't know exactly *how* to get more creativity in us.

The use of our imagination and the ability to come up with great ideas goes well beyond artistic work. If you ask a neuroscientist, they'll likely give you a long list of the ways creativity benefits the brain. That brain connection makes this all seem scientific, yet the act of *practicing* creativity can be so basic and simple.

So, let's not complicate it!

HOW CREATIVITY CAN MAKE LIFE BETTER

I think we can all agree that there are many benefits to being creative. Whether we're parenting children or managing a technical group, we'll be presented with challenges that require us to be creative.

Writing this piece required me to step outside of my comfort zone and embrace creativity! The biggest benefit I witness in these situations is the pure joy of making something and the way it can enhance all areas of your life, at work and at home.

Consider this: your job is no longer a separate part of your life the way it used to be. Our work and personal lives are becoming more and more integrated. Flexible work schedules have given us more access to lifestyle benefits if we take advantage of all the small opportunities.

Given these advantages, wouldn't it make sense to discover yourself in more areas, so you can enjoy the best of both worlds? Being more creative helps you grow as a person which can help you in your work.

We may have lost our creative spark somewhere along the road from childhood to adulthood, but just like physical exercise, it's never too late to get it back. The more we practice, the more it flows. And so we explore, experiment and try not to cry when most of our creative attempts go wrong.

Your creative endeavors may or may not work out, but you need to be okay with that if you want to grow. Becoming comfortable with uncertainty is just one benefit from practicing creativity. Think about how much better off we are if we can accept uncertainty in so many areas of our lives (unless you're undergoing brain surgery of course!).

JUST DO IT!

To be inspired, you have to get inspired. And to get inspired, you have to make it a point to do something that might lead you in that direction. Creativity doesn't just happen—you have to make it happen.

As elusive as creativity is, it does require that we put it on the calendar. Make a date with creativity. Maybe gather a few people together and have someone lead the group in small, simple creative tasks. However you decide to move forward, have a plan and do something. Get dirty if you must but please have fun creating something!

Find something to wake up for and be excited about. Are you doing anything that's just about the joy of creation and not necessarily tied to money or work? When we start forgetting about the things that light our fire, we die a little inside and it's up to us to get that spark back.

In the words of Tim Ferris:

"Strive for excitement! Instead of asking 'What do I want or what are my goals' ask 'What would excite me?'"

Feed your soul and create the passion that is critical to enriching your life and the lives of those around you. Let's all take a more child-like, relaxed approach to this and simply create for the sake enjoyment. Anything more is just a bonus!

MARIA GATLING

Maria Gatling is a visual artist whose drive is to help others tap into their creative side.

She feels strongly that practicing creativity stimulates leaders, problem solvers, and lifelong learners. But most importantly, it brings personal satisfaction, meaning, and joy to our lives.

Maria has written and composed two workbooks, *Project 52* and *Coffee Break Creativity Grande*.

Her work is a simple invitation to rediscover your creative awesomeness and bring back the joyful, creative force we had as children. Maria's seven-word bio: "I help others find inspiration to create."

◉ | LOCATION:
Austin, Texas

✉ | EMAIL:
marygatling@mac.com

🖥 | WEB SITE:
https://mariagatling.com

✎ | AUTHOR OF:
Project 52
and
Coffee Break Creativity Grande

🏆 | SPECIALTIES:
- Creativity workshops
- Guest presenter for events, such as a retreat, conference, or meeting
- Facilitate meetings
- One-on-one creative coaching

"I *am* a team player, I just play for the other team."

COULD IT REALLY BE THIS SIMPLE?

KIMBERLY WIEFLING

Many threats that businesses face are completely and utterly human. According to one study published in MIT Sloan's management journal[1] a while back, the most common causes for failure in the global teams that they studied (over 80 percent self-reported as failing!) were:

- **Lack of trusting relationships.**

- **Failure to overcome communication barriers** (and this is *not* limited to language and culture!).

- **Unclear goals.**

- **Misalignment between individual and team priorities.**

---

1   https://sloanreview.mit.edu/article/building-an-effective-global-business-team/

Look at this list. Whose responsibility is it to ensure that teams build strong, trusting relationships and work together effectively toward clear, shared goals upon which all team members are aligned? This is entirely a failure of leadership! (Notice I didn't say management. There's a big difference between leadership and management, and I've never met anyone who liked being managed!)

Sure, there are other contributing factors, but let's not be so quick to forgive this tragic absence of effective leadership in the global work environment. Even a brief peek into the inner workings of many organizations reveals that they are not teams, but merely groups of people working together. Their managers are not leaders, and their organizations are dysfunctional by design, thanks to power poisoning and hierarchies that breed what have come to be known as "bossholes." (Yup, there's a whole new word for people who suck their employees' will to live!) Their cynicism-inducing values may be posted on the wall, but unless they'll fire their best engineer for violating those principles, these values are worthless—even a liability to a healthy organizational culture.

With only a fraction of workers truly committed to their work, many organizations achieve success through a combination of heroics, diving catches, miracles, and luck. Some of these accidental achievers ask me, "Kimberly, if our company is so screwed up, why are we successful?" Why, indeed! Lucky for them, most of their peers are equally mediocre.

Surely the people responsible for such wasteful misery would recognize their toxic—and sometimes "talk-sick"—impact on their colleagues and change their behavior, right? Unfortunately, often no one feels responsible for this needless suffering. When I work with individual employees, they say, "Sure, Kimberly, we want to make the changes you're suggesting, but it's our managers who are really the cause of these problems." And when I challenge managers on these workplace issues they often point to their executives as the real cause of their difficulties. Executives then point to the CEO, who—heartbroken to think that they might be to blame for this tragic loss of opportunity—confides that the chairman, board, investors, shareholders, or other influences are at the root of these problems.

Let's all get busy doing the real work of management—leading! Could we do something more strategic first thing in the morning other than checking email? Might we find better ways to spend our time besides meaningless meetings where the only thing that we decide is to meet again? If so, we'd have an excellent opportunity to dramatically improve business results and even—dare I say—enjoy our work. Start with a purpose beyond profit and a mission that matters. Implement commonsense people leadership and business management approaches proven to deliver results predictably and repeatedly. Recognize and sincerely appreciate people's contributions to the organization. This practical approach has the power to truly engage employees, inviting and inspiring people to be strongly committed to shared goals that would be impossible for any individual to achieve but are inevitable for a true team.

I don't expect reading this to change you. If knowing how to do something were enough, we'd all be rich and thin! There's always some reason why well-intentioned, educated, experienced professionals are doing the opposite of what they know makes sense. Frequently, it's because they are really busy and can't possibly do what needs to be done until someone *else* changes first—usually their boss or someone in a different department. A well-researched book called *The Knowing-Doing Gap* was written by two Stanford University professors who noticed that their colleagues at the Stanford Graduate School of Business didn't follow their *own* teachings when they *themselves* led companies.

What is the source of the gap between knowing and doing?

- **Learned Helplessness.** "It's not my fault!" and "They are doing it to me" thinking.

- **Fear of Failure.** If you're not allowed to fail, you must be very careful what you start.

- **Aversion to Planning.** As I've mentioned, given a choice, people prefer not to plan—at *all*!

- **Instinct for Competition.** A win-lose frame is the first assumption that many people make in any situation involving another person, even when win-win can yield more benefits to them.

Knowing *how*, by itself, changes *nothing*! Over 70 percent of business failures have been attributed to an inability to execute. Doing what has been proven effective by decades of experience, such as healthy leadership, teams, project management, organizational culture, beats a great theory any day.

If we acknowledge the dark side of organizations and our own contributions to them, we can create a future where individuals, teams, and organizations generate great results by design rather than by chance. Investors might be happy with a 10 percent success rate for the companies they invest in, but do you really want to accept those odds? You needn't. We can do better.

You may be asking yourself, "Could it really be this simple?" Simple, yes. Easy, no. Using this approach, you can make what seems impossible merely difficult, then possible, and enable your team to achieve together what no one could do alone. With so much to gain, not only for your people but for our world, we need to *keep going*! And when we do fail, let's fail for new and more exciting reasons!

KIMBERLY WIEFLING

Kimberly helps people achieve what seems impossible but is merely difficult. She's the founder of Wiefling Consulting and co-founder of Silicon Valley Alliances. She wrote a project management book that has been popular globally for over a decade, *Scrappy Project Management*, that was also published in Japanese. She's also the executive editor of a series, Scrappy Guides. Her mentor, Dr. Edgar Schein, wrote the foreword to her book, *Inspired Organizational Cultures*. Her expertise includes leadership, team effectiveness, project management, and organizational culture. Kimberly loves to engage with people committed to solving global problems profitably and making a positive difference on Planet Earth.

◉ | LOCATION:
Northern California

✉ | EMAIL:
kimberly@wiefling.com

🖥 | WEB SITES:
https://kimberlywiefling.com/
https://wiefling.com/
https://siliconvalleyalliances.com/

✏ | AUTHOR OF:
Scrappy Project Management
and
Inspired Organizational Cultures

🏆 | SPECIALTIES:
- Scrappy Project Management
  https://scrappyprojectmanagement.com/
- Leadership and Team Effectiveness
  https://possibilitiestoolbox.com/
- Design Thinking/Creativity/Innovation
  https://scrappydesignthinking.com/
- Organizational Culture/DNA
  https://inspiredcompanyculture.com/

👤 | AVAILABLE FOR:
Consulting and workshop facilitation.

"Bad news. Another one of our employees
has been poached."

WORKING HUMAN 101: IF YOU THANK THEM, THEY WILL STAY

DEREK IRVINE

Let's look at the current state of the American workplace: unemployment is the lowest in fifty years, and there's a massive shift in how work gets done. It's more team-based, more collaborative, and the movement to bring humanity back to the workplace continues gaining momentum.

Not to mention, much of the workforce is made up of millennials who have entirely different expectations about work. Gone are the days of command-and-control leadership; instead people want autonomy and meaning—and to belong.

You know what they say about change? It's good. And this is all good. But there is one question hanging in the balance for many organizations:

in a climate where jobs are there for the taking, how do you set your brand apart? How do you become the place people choose over others? And how do you build a culture where people don't just stay, but stay *and* do the best work of their lives?

It's simple, really. And once I tell you and offer irrefutable data points, you'll probably sit there and think to yourself, "Well, duh. That's a no-brainer." It is, but sometimes things are so obvious that you need someone to point them out. So, what's the secret to retaining and nurturing your people (and your business)?

Just add gratitude.

THE POWER OF GRATITUDE

Great organizations know that the more gratitude in a company, the better it performs. It's been proven time and again that peer-to-peer recognition changes the giver and creates the best kind of ripple effect. Work cultures where peers can recognize each other for the work they do every day have employees who are:

- **52 percent less likely to leave.**

- **32 percent more likely to perform at a higher level.**

- **73 percent more likely to go above and beyond*.**

But it's not just gratitude that does this alone—it's about the reach, frequency, and value of that gratitude.

Peer-to-peer recognition transcends teams, departments, and titles—anyone can recognize anyone, not just manager-down. And it includes all employees, from the entry-level worker to the CEO. In other words, if 80 percent of your people are using the platform, your reach is 80 percent. And the more recognition going around, the more human connections are being made and the more collaboration, engagement, and innovation is happening.

It's a similar story with the amount of rewards people receive. Turnover is cut in half when people receive between seven and ten recognition moments a year, year-over-year performance increases with five or more awards a year, and engagement and appreciation increase with between one and two awards per quarter.*

RECOGNITION = HAPPY EMPLOYEES

Of course, to truly build a culture rooted in gratitude that will thrive in this job seeker's market, you need investment. We all know you have to spend money to make money.

And according to research, programs funded at 1 percent or more of payroll are 86 percent more likely to be rated as good or excellent. These programs tend to be aligned with the organization's people strategy.* And since an organization's people strategy is often tied to important business metrics, like retention rate of critical employees, strength of company values, and employee happiness, a recognition program to shed light on these metrics is invaluable.

The data don't lie. Done right, gratitude and recognition work—it all comes down to simply treating people well, with dignity and appreciation. Like human beings. It's not revolutionary or rocket science. It seems silly that we need to remind ourselves to practice humanity at work, doesn't it? Here's to a future where we no longer need to. It'll be here sooner than you think. Maybe it already is.

---

*   Based on customer data from the Workhuman® Analytics & Research Institute and research done in collaboration with SHRM.

DEREK IRVINE

As senior vice president, client strategy and consulting at Workhuman®, Derek leads the company's consulting division. In this role, he helps clients—including some of world's most admired companies—leverage proven recognition strategies and best practices to elevate employee engagement, increase retention, and improve bottom-line results. In addition to leading consulting services for Workhuman, Derek also oversaw the company's marketing and rewards functions for a decade.

Derek is one of the world's foremost experts on employee recognition and engagement, helping business leaders set a higher vision and ambition for their company culture. As a renowned speaker and co-author of *Winning with a Culture of Recognition* and *The Power of Thanks*, he teaches HR leaders how to use recognition to proactively manage company culture. His viewpoints and writings are also regularly featured across major HR publications including *Workspan*, *HR Magazine*, *HR Executive*, *Talent Management*, and *Workforce Management*.

🌐 | LOCATION:
Spain

✉ | EMAIL:
derek.irvine@workhuman.com

🖥 | WEB SITE:
https://workhuman.com

✏ | CO-AUTHOR OF:
Winning with a Culture of Recognition
and
The Power of Thanks

🏆 | SPECIALTIES:
- Employee recognition
- Employee engagement
- Building workplace cultures rooted in gratitude

👤 | AVAILABLE FOR:
Radio and TV interviews, public speaking and consulting.

"You just *had* to have a corner office!"

HUMBITION

LYNETTE CAMPBELL

Imagine touring the corporate office of a large, highly successful organization you've heard about. It's extremely productive and profitable, the employees are highly engaged, and customers rave about its products and services.

As you move through the building and hear what the tour guide is saying, you begin to realize the way you previously thought about "status" within organizations shows up differently here. It's surprising.

You learn these details:

- **Every on-site employee has a cubicle the same size, with furniture and equipment appropriate for the requirements of the position.** There are no offices.

- **Cubicles are arranged, so no one has a more advantageous view.** In fact, outdoor views are designed as open spaces for group discussions.

- **All decor is identical on each floor.** There is no special top floor for executives with thicker carpeting, more valuable artwork, expensive desks, or ornate chandeliers.

- **Phones, company vehicles, and other equipment are given to employees based upon demonstrated need and job requirements, not title.**

- **All employees are visible and accessible.** No "gatekeepers" exist to prevent you from speaking to higher-level employees, although common courtesy prevails.

- **The only trophies and awards displayed are for the entire organization's achievements.** Even though it has a healthy sales division, no "salesman of the year" or "employee of the year" plaques or pictures are on the wall – because no individual awards are given.

- **Team achievements and organizational achievements receive top billing in the company newsletter, and community service by teammates is showcased regularly.**

- **Every desirable parking space is chosen annually through a voluntary lottery.**

- **Everyone has the opportunity to apply for any open position.** Promotions do not exist. Interviews and selection for a position involves not only the candidate's future leader, but also a carefully chosen and diverse group of people who hold relevant related positions. Depending upon who is applying, the final interview may be conducted by the candidate's team, and they are asked to give input into the decision.

- **Incentives are given on a team basis, awarding an equal percentage of pay to each team member, based upon overall customer results and profit.**

- **Recognition for high performance is generous, simple, and given tax free.**

- **In meetings, all team members have a voice, and in important decisional meetings, a neutral facilitator prepares and leads the process to ensure collaboration and consensus.**

The organization has not completely removed power and status. What remains? In this particular organization:

- **There is a known hierarchy with titles and commensurate pay.** Everyone understands all employees can be graded higher and paid more, based upon their job requirements and the increasing responsibility they are assuming in the organization.

- **Power, while downplayed, still exists as responsibility and accountability (the buck stops here!).** And, people report to each other, coach and rate performance, and determine merit compensation.

Even so, the tour guide says, employees are satisfied because of the lack of status symbols and promotional power. There is higher trust and considerably less "we" versus "they."

As you leave the tour, you wonder: does this unique structure take away the motivation for performance? Are healthy ambition and high-performance still possible in an organization like this? Can people be humble and not pursue status, yet remain engaged and ambitious ("humbition") at the same time?

I submit that not only is it possible and thriving in many organizations, I believe this type of culture is going to become more and more necessary to engage and retain employees of all ages - especially Millennials.

So how could an already-established organization begin to implement a humbitious culture?

It must start with healthy, brutally honest discussions and complete agreement at the highest levels of the organization. Everyone must agree.

Giving up the old definition of status is admittedly a huge mind shift—turning around hundreds (even thousands!) of years of people believing that ambition, effort, and savvy political maneuvers lead to increasing power and status. (Think of kings and their court or the military.)

In this new type of organizational culture, everyone (and their families, who also have influence on the employee) must "make meaning" differently as they pursue their career. Instead of thinking about advancement that includes the awarding of showy status symbols and power, ambition and performance is instead channeled to finding purpose, making a contribution, the thrill of collaboration, and serving others. Performing well and gaining expertise would instead lead to more responsibility, higher pay, and increased respect.

Finally, the entire executive team must create explicit, intentional agreements on how humbition will look in the culture. It cannot be phony and must be more than lip service. Commitment will show up immediately in words and actions. Humbition must be expected from all.

There are many more details that must be thought through.

And, part of the humility is explaining that the organization is constantly piloting and there will be missteps as people learn this new way of being in an organization. Feedback and forgiveness is essential. But, in the end, trust, authenticity, engagement, and cultural health will increase.

Would you be willing to work in a humbitious culture?

LYNETTE CAMPBELL

Lynette Campbell has been passionate about helping individuals, teams, and organizations develop and thrive throughout her entire career. As an executive and senior consultant in large financial and hospitality organizations for twenty-five years, she brings a wealth of practical experience to such topics as engagement, change management, culture change, recognition, and employee well-being. Lynette holds a master's in Organizational Performance from Drake University, the CPLP from ASTD, as well as many certifications.

⊕ | LOCATION:

Omaha, Nebraska

✉ | EMAIL:

Lynette.Campbell2019@outlook.com

🏆 | SPECIALTIES:

- Culture consultation
- Engagement
- Employee well-being
- Recognition
- Facilitation

👤 | AVAILABLE FOR:

Culture consulting and speaking.

© MARK ANDERSON, WWW.ANDERTOONS.COM

"I've told you before - you do the interpretive stuff
on your own time!"

WHY EVERY COMPANY NEEDS A DREAM PROGRAM

DAN RALPHS

Let's face it, the relationship between employer and employee is inherently adversarial.

Why? It's simple. We trust someone to the degree that we believe that they have our best interests at heart. And employees typically don't believe that their bosses care about anything but the company's bottom line.

Think of it this way: I trust my wife because I know she loves me and is as likely, if not more likely, to take care of my needs ahead of her own. But I don't trust the shady car salesman because I'm pretty sure his only goal is to line his own pocketbook.

With rare exception, employees know they are valued only to the degree that they are valuable. They know that the company comes first—so everything spoken on behalf of the company inherently comes with an air of distrust.

It's no wonder, then, that programs designed to care for and serve the employees tend to flounder.

Perhaps an employer offers a development program to help their employees grow in their careers. But can you see how, in the light of distrust, that can sound like a friend offering friendship classes and calling it "generosity?" It can come across as self-serving and disingenuous.

EMPLOYERS AS TRUSTED CONFIDANTES

This is a sad story. Sadder still is the fact that most leaders I meet genuinely care for their employees. They authentically want to see their employees happy, well paid, and successful. So as caring leaders, how can we break through the deeply seated script that implies employers are only in it for themselves?

In 2013, I was hired to be a Dream Coach at a small software company called Infusionsoft. It may sound crazy, but I was told my job was to help our employees identify, articulate, and accomplish their personal dreams, whatever those might be.

As you might imagine, I quickly became a trusted guy. After all, I was a corporate fairly godmother, there to coach individuals toward their dreams. These included dreams like traveling, starting their own businesses, and even adopting a child. But something I didn't expect was the number of beleaguered managers who confided in me that they wished they had my job.

That's when I realized the magic that I had experienced as a Dream Coach should be shared with our leaders. What if leadership in the organization could enjoy that same level of trust? So, we went to work to create the *Dream Leadership Certification*.

In this training, we invited leaders to add "Dream Coach" to their list of roles and gave them a simple coaching model to help them have a new kind of conversation. Soon, leaders all over the organization were asking their employees in a caring way about their dreams.

CREATING AN ENVIRONMENT OF TRUST

Given the nature of trust, it's no surprise that we saw the level of trust, engagement, and ownership increase on the teams where leaders were implementing these practices.

For the first time, the agenda of the individual employee had a safe place to express itself. For the first time, employees believed that perhaps the organization had their best interests in mind. For the first time, they saw leaders as advocates and not just bosses.

Some leaders feared that if they didn't hold a hard line, it would give employees the idea that they were soft or encourage an attitude of employee entitlement. They wondered, when will we get any work done when our employees are focused on their own dreams and not the company vision?

But it turns out that the opposite was true. The employees, whose relationship with their leader changed from transactional to authentic, were more likely to work harder, be more committed, and give discretionary effort to the team. After all, I am far more likely to serve and sacrifice for my wife than for the car salesman.

As a leader, if it feels like you're pulling teeth or trust is hard to come by, you need to ask yourself if your employees have sufficient reason to believe that you're on their side. Do their agendas, goals, and even their dreams matter to you? Do you genuinely care about their happiness and fulfillment?

Until you demonstrate that you're in it for them, it's sure to be an uphill battle to get them to be in it for you.

DAN RALPHS

Dan is the founder of Dream Leadership Consulting and is one of the world's foremost experts on unlocking the power of dreaming.

He has an amazing ability to help people discover their own dreams and learn how to go after them. His realistic approach to dreaming recognizes that dreaming is not a "magic pill" but rather a new way of thinking about our ability to create.

Before founding Dream Coach, Dan was the facilitator of the Dreaming Program at Infusionsoft (a small software company in Chandler, Arizona), where he helped its employees to identify, articulate, and accomplish their dreams.

He also is the creator of the Dream Leader Certification course, in which he has supported over 100 leaders from all over the world to become Dream Leaders to those they lead. Together they have helped their people accomplish dreams like buying a first home, riding elephants in Thailand, and starting a foundation to help mothers facing infant loss. Between Dan and the Dream Leaders, he has certified there are thousands who have been awakened to their dreams and their ability to achieve them.

⊕ | LOCATION:
Gilbert, Arizona

✉ | EMAIL:
dan@thedreamblog.com

▢ | WEB SITE:

https://dreamleadershipconsulting.com

🏆 | SPECIALTIES:
- Dream Leadership certification
- Keynote speaking
- Multipliers certified
- Small business executive coaching (7–8 Figure Growth)

👤 | AVAILABLE FOR:
Culture consulting, keynote speaking, executive coaching, and strategic planning.

"Sure, I'm scared. But the ichthyologist in me is kind of thrilled."

HYPNOTICALLY RESOLVING CONFLICT IS BLOCKING YOUR COMPANY'S GROWTH

DAWNA JONES

For decades, conflict resolution has been the go-to for companies. Traditionally they've used the classic flight, fight, or flee reactions as the patterns for automatic responses. However, a conflict resolution approach is outdated.

Hypnotically resolve tension (which usually involves ignoring or avoiding the conversation), and you kill the value of diversity. An unintended side effect is that the most destructive behaviors are left unchecked to devastate workplace health. These behaviors include bullying, exerting pressure to conform, forcing achievement of metrics while sacrificing the health of employees and customers' well-being, signaling weak skills, strength, and conviction.

Conflict is simply energy seeking a direction. In *Warriors of the Heart*, global visionary Danaan Perry described it as spiraling up or down. The flow is either generative in effect or destructive.

Spiral up and you co-create better solutions using the value of diverse perspectives. Ignore or avoid conflict, and it dives down a destructive path, blocking creative contribution.

IGNORING CONFLICT RUINS RESILIENCY

The hypnotic routine that many companies default to—particularly under pressure—sabotages company resiliency. Executives, particularly in the older demographic, are complicit in the failure to adapt. Advancing internal capacity is sacrificed for short-term profit motives, ignoring long-term business sustainability. Relentlessly focused on achieving the next quarterly report, decision-makers' readiness for today's realities are blind to the risk of doing nothing.

Traditionally hierarchical organizations with centralized authority and decision-making invest much time maintaining a false perfection. It's costly in terms of human and organizational expression because the focus is on suppressing the dark side, which gives it power over interpersonal dynamics. The difficult issues and conversations stay hidden, undermining personal and organizational growth.

For business cultures to support accurate decisions, bold leadership and healthy take-your-whole-self-to-work workplaces, mastering conflict resolution skills is vital. The more skilled you are, the more you can redirect tensions from tearing key relationships apart to redirecting and refocusing that same energy into both innovation and growth, shifting the focus from self-preservation to achieving organizational goals.

Companies are racing to oblivion out of pure complacency, the twin partner of indifference.

HAVING THE COURAGE TO RISE ABOVE

Leaders rely on courage to rise above assumptions that worked in the past. The right brand of leadership courage recognizes that doing what's easy won't achieve the best result. It equips senior-level decision-makers with the humanity and empathy needed to creatively transform a company from a paradigm of exploitation to value creation.

Utilizing conflict requires a capacity to self-observe, then self-correct. It necessitates entering into conversations with a different mind-set. Core personal power centered in trust fuels more responsible and competent leadership capable of converting conflict from a downside disaster into an upside learning, value-added for all involved.

Changing the quality of conversations within an organization improves the quality and capacity of relationships. This creates cultural equity where a safety net of trust and learning supports calculated risk-taking.

MAKING THE RIGHT CHOICE

At heart is choice; the choice to use conflict as a teacher or to back away and defer learning to another day. Micro-adjustments, such as how you listen or how you balance questions with observations, ripple rapidly through the social neural network in a company.

One shift in stance and demonstrable skill—especially at senior levels—can ignite the desire and aspiration for a workplace culture where you can take your whole self to work without risking social and psychological safety.

Unfortunately, leaders in authority positions are notoriously stubborn about hanging on to control, even when it kills the company's initiative and foresight.

Companies running on authority instead of shared leadership are not equipped to deal positively and constructively with conflict. It will take courageous and empathic leaders to say what needs to be said, make toxic workplaces safe for growth, witness the flow of energy, and know when the tough questions need to be asked and answered collectively.

It calls upon leaders to access a deeper skill set and way of moving through the world that rises above the need for approval and taps into their core essence.

DAWNA JONES

Dawna Jones helps decision-makers at every level use complex challenges to shift perspective, freeing suppressed human and organizational potential. Her customized learning programs advance skills in decision-making and accelerate responsiveness and resilience. Adept in perceiving the deep dynamics and working with emergent events, Dawna's strategic insights provide clarity. Learning experiences draw on novelty, a profound understanding of the biology of the human spirit and the sciences.

Podcaster and high-impact speaker, Dawna wrote *Decision Making for Dummies*;[1] contributed to *The Intelligence of the Cosmos* by Ervin Laszlo,[2] and co-authored *From Hierarchy to High Performance*.[3] Listen to her Inspirational Insights podcast[4] and find her on LinkedIn.

---

1   https://amzn.to/39JCVKV
2   https://bit.ly/2sS7pKg
3   https://amzn.to/2tUnVKa
4   https://shows.pippa.io/insight-to-action-inspirational-insights-podcast/

❾ | LOCATION:

Vancouver, B.C., Canada | Worldwide

✉ | EMAIL:

info@dawna-jones.co

🖥 | WEB SITES:

http://Dawna-Jones.co

https://amzn.to/2T1bTbZ

https://bit.ly/2ZUwekK

https://bit.ly/2FpaMea

✏ | AUTHOR OF:

Decision Making for Dummies

🏆 | SPECIALTIES:

- Transforming personal capacity to work with complexity
- Organizational transformation
- Tackling global issues
- Decision-making
- Deep dynamics blocking or supporting higher purpose
- Workplace health
- Using adversity to strengthen resilience personally/organizationally

👤 | AVAILABLE FOR:

Speaking, facilitating, custom workshop design and delivery, and strategic mentoring for executive leaders.

"It's not that you're under-performing so much as
you're over-failing."

ONE-ON-ONES ARE REALLY FOR NO ONE

JOSHUA VANDE KROL

How often do you go home and ask your partner or significant other: "How am I performing in our relationship?" Or meet with your children and listen to their feedback on how you can be a better parent? I'd wager it's pretty much never.

But when we get to work, most of us want to have a regularly scheduled meeting with our boss to hear that we're doing a good job. If we don't get it, that little voice in our head tells us that we're failing and we need to step it up.

Unfortunately, our current institutional processes of providing this desired feedback leaves us unsatisfied and wanting more.

DOES THE BOSS REALLY KNOW BEST?

Your work success is often dependent on what the boss thinks of your work. But other than a couple conversations with you every week, they often aren't privy to what you do or how well you do it, right?

Often, companies have overcrowded teams where a boss manages too many people and a single yearly performance is the only time feedback is shared. "Good" bosses provide feedback more often, but still only capture a small percentage of the actual work performed during that period. The typical boss, especially in a small business, rarely or never performs these one-on-ones and often only does so when the employee asks for a raise.

If you are one of those "good" bosses, your goal is a happy workforce that's highly productive with a retention rate through the roof, right? If so, stop doing what you were taught in corporate America. You need to stop inserting these artificial people reviews—even if your team is asking for it. High retention rates are not dependent on these, period.

LEARNING THE HARD WAY

As the COO of an early stage start-up that uses a self-managed methodology, our company had the typical gap in our feedback loop. Because self-managed companies believe that people do not manage people (they manage commitments), the typical performance review didn't apply. However, we found that our modified team reviews didn't work any better than those in a traditional company.

For the same reason that one-on-ones in traditional companies don't work, a team format where peers provide feedback didn't change the results; people were still unhappy with the fact that they didn't get the feedback they wanted.

We discovered that forced time with someone else to share your review of their individual performance is rife with confrontation. Many of us are introverts and the idea of having to be honest with our assessment of a team member is too uncomfortable to follow through with.

Instead, consider this.

REVIEW THE WORK – *NOT* THE PERSON

Stop making these reviews personal; it's about the work.

Here's an example. A review of the work is a standard and natural practice for most development teams. Code is submitted by a developer and reviewed by another developer prior to completion. The developers listen to one another, provide suggestions, and after the *work* approval of their peers, the item moves forward to the next step in the release cycle.

In this work review, teammates can both learn and come together in practice. There is not a judgment issued against the person; it's a product evaluation created by the individual. The person then feels the *direct* value of their contribution to the team's purpose.

This is easy advice if you are a member of a development team, right? While this is not a natural, recurring scenario for most other teams in business, it should be. Here are a couple examples of where this might come into play:

- **Sales teams conducting demo reviews with one another. Record them and review them!**

- **Opportunity/lead reviews of both closed won and closed lost opportunities for both sales and customer success.**

- **Customer support personnel conducting a training session review.**

- **Customer success and sales personnel conducting a kick-off review of a customer kick-off and how well the transition went.**

- **Content reviews in marketing teams.**

- **Communication reviews with team leads.**

- **New hire onboarding review with your hiring team.**

Bottom line—if you are part of a team, you are heading toward a goal together and producing a "product" that needs review.

TEAM RETROSPECTIVES ARE A WIN

The term *retrospective* became popular in software teams employing agile principles and scrum methodologies. It should be considered a standard for all teams where work in a period is evaluated and the targeted measures of success are reviewed and discussed.

Whether the sales goal for the month by unit or revenue was realized or not, the team still discusses its performance. These retrospectives can be as simple as *"What are the one or two things that we should do differently next time?"* and *"What are the one or two things that we should keep doing?"* to more complex retrospectives with a more detailed analysis.

This is a review of the overall team and how it's performing. It's a time where the team can meet and reflect on their work and measure it against their goal. It's a chance to celebrate their success and learn from the journey.

BE ORGANIC AND NATURAL

In short, stop trying to insert artificial meetings for individual reviews. Be organic and natural in your work relationships, mirroring what we do in the rest of our lives, and get rid of that corporate, stilted process for finding your value.

JOSHUA VANDE KROL

Joshua Vande Krol is a technology operationalist at heart with a breadth of experience in multiple industries and in a variety of organizational sizes. He's led teams in their development of technology solutions for multiple companies and fields, including Microsoft, PIMCO, Kaiser Permanente, Gartner, and Tableau. He has implemented best practices of business processes through experience and certifications in Lean, Six Sigma, Agile, and Scrum. Josh is a certified Scrum Master and  Product Owner and is currently helping Hubb move beyond an early stage start-up to their next level of maturity as their Chief Operations Officer.

His recent experience includes four start-ups in five different industries, ranging from the travel industry, healthcare, finance, hospitality, and manufacturing, often joining the company as one of the first employee(s) or pursuing his entrepreneurial spirit as a co-owner/co-founder.

🌐 | LOCATION:

Vancouver, Washington

✉ | EMAIL:

jvandekrol@comcast.net

"I think I'm most interested in hearing about the part
of your resume titled 'Stuff I Totally Rocked.'"

WORKING CLASS HEROES

THOMAS MCCOY

While there is a lot of literature available on the topic of engagement, the truth is that without interacting with different socioeconomic groups, it's difficult to understand what really engages the workforce.

In an effort to gain insight, I recently took a job for eight weeks that paid $13.35/hr. The hours were from 6:30 a.m. to 3:00 p.m., with two paid fifteen-minute breaks and thirty minutes (unpaid) for lunch. That was quite a change for me as a consultant, chief researcher, and president of the Employee Engagement Institute.

The work took place in an office environment, but the workflow was similar to an assembly line. It involved extended concentration, rapid pattern recognition, repetitive motion, and in-depth knowledge of the details in a 400-page instruction manual.

This was a job that required intelligence, commitment, and physical effort. There were aggressive speed and quality metrics. We were frequently reminded that missing either one of them was grounds for termination. Over time, the work resulted in repetitive motion injuries for almost all of the workers.

It was the type of work that is performed by 70 percent of the population over twenty-five years of age, people without a college degree. These are the people who do most of the physical work in this country. The preponderance of workers on this job could be classified as belonging to a minority group, which in this situation, made them a majority and made me a minority. For them, this was life.

Sprinkled among them were college-educated workers who were laid off from some company and traumatized by the fact that, being over forty, they no longer fit into the white-collar workforce. For them, this was a last chance.

The onboarding experience was worse than bad and, as a result, it established negative expectations. Once on the floor, the supervisory skills were minimal and, perhaps because the work was seasonal, leadership was nonexistent.

As a result, there was a high degree of turnover—but mostly from the new employees. The core of employees with over two years of repeat employment was rock solid. Why was that?

The work itself was intellectually challenging, and it turned out that the employees took pride in the fact that they could master the complex set of rules outlined in the manual and develop a unique skill set. Surprisingly, the culture on the floor was one of camaraderie. Even with aggressive productivity goals, my fellow employees were supportive and encouraging. Everyone I asked was glad to provide guidance and the time to help a newcomer. The informal motto on the floor was "We are all in this together."

This local culture, this social environment in which the work took place, had evolved in the workplace, belonged to the workplace and was separate from the organization's culture. (The higher one rose through the ranks, the more toxic the culture became.)

As I interacted with my co-workers, I observed that the culture on the floor was due to the fact that the work provided a sense of dignity.

By developing the ability to perform a difficult job well, one earned the recognition and respect of one's peers.

Here was evidence of the underlying foundation for engagement. Work that enables a person to perform and contribute and in doing so develop a sense of self-respect, provides a sense of dignity. Lacking any demonstrations of appreciation from the leadership, workers developed dignity through the acknowledgment and respect of their peers. The workers honored the work even if the leadership didn't.

Without interacting with different socioeconomic groups, it's difficult to understand what engages them. It turns out that we all want the same thing—*dignity and respect.*

THOMAS MCCOY

Thomas McCoy is a coach, consultant, and president of the Employee Engagement Institute.[1] He offers clients the possibility of developing a high-involvement, high-performance company by connecting employees to the customers, the financials, the processes, and the company culture. This provides the opportunity to gain and retain market share and increase profits with a smooth-running organization.

In 1993, Mr. McCoy established himself as a pioneer in the field of employee engagement with his breakthrough book, *Compensation and Motivation*.[2] He now has over thirty-five years of applied experience and has provided services to over 250 private and public companies in the US, Europe, and South America. Leaders start seeing business results in as little as sixty days.

He has been featured in the *Wall Street Journal*, quoted in *Newsweek*, and nominated for SHRM's Michael J. Losey award for his work in the field of Human Resources. He developed and taught a two-day seminar at George Washington University called *How to Develop a High-Involvement, High-Performance Culture*.

Mr. McCoy is a member of MENSA. He holds a Lean/Six Sigma certificate from Villanova University, a coaching certification from the Johnston Institute, and is a graduate from the University of Minnesota. He is a Marine Corps veteran and a volunteer board member for the nonprofit Support KC. He and his wife Cathy are the parents of two young men.

---

1   http://employeeengagementinstitute.com
2   https://amzn.to/2tz9D15

◉ | LOCATION:
Kansas City, Missouri

✉ | EMAIL:
tjmccoy@EmpEng.com

🖵 | WEB SITE:
http://EmpEng.com

✎ | AUTHOR OF:
Compensation and Motivation

🏆 | SPECIALTIES:
- Culture and engagement strategy development
- Incentive pay design and implementation
- ScoreCard development
- Culture and engagement education
- Culture and engagement measurement
- Quality of Work Experience Survey (QWE)
- The Applied Employee Engagement System™

👤 | AVAILABLE FOR:
Culture coaching, engagement consulting, incentive pay design, and implementation support for the Applied Employee Engagement System™.

"We're reorganizing our infrastructure. Everyone move two chairs to the left."

WHY REINVENTING ORGANIZATIONS IS ABOUT MORE THAN JUST CHANGING STRUCTURES

LISA GILL

It's no secret that the way we're working isn't working. Even the most dyed-in-the-wool organizations are acknowledging that they need to adapt and transition from—as author Chuck Blakeman puts it—the "Industrial Age" to the "Participation Age."

However, most people are focusing on structures and busying themselves with installing the latest trend, whether it's Agile, Lean, Beyond Budgeting, Results-Only Work Environments, Holacracy, Sociocracy, or some other system.

Structures are important and certainly need to be redesigned, but changing structures alone is not enough.

CHANGING MINDS, CHANGING WORKPLACES

Miki Kashtan, author and international teacher of Nonviolent Communication, describes two other shifts[1] that need to happen in order for us to achieve a new, more purposeful level of collaboration in our organizations. They are shifts, not of the structural kind, but of the human kind—in being, in relating, in mind-sets.

First, those who have (or have had) structural power, for instance, managers need to unlearn their top-down tendencies and learn instead to welcome new perspectives and trust others with radical responsibility.

Second, those who don't have (or haven't had) structural power—in this case, employees—need to unlearn their bottom-up tendencies. They must overcome fear and deference and ask for what they need, daring to question or challenge or propose. In other words, both managers and employees need to shift their mind-sets and ways of being to one of distributed leadership and shared power.

Mary Parker Follett was writing about this as early as the 1920s, calling it a shift from "power over" to "power with."

A NEW PARADIGM OF SHARED POWER

These shifts will be challenging because in some cases they go against decades of "power over" conditioning from our families, schools, societies, and workplaces. But without shifts occurring in these two places, as Miki describes, any attempts to become an agile organization—or anything else—will be short-lived and surface level.

You could characterize this human shift as transforming the dynamic between managers and nonmanagers from a parent-child dynamic (where the manager is responsible and the one that problem-solves, decides, etc.)

---

1   Listen to my full conversation with Miki Kashtan for the Leadermorphosis podcast here: http://leadermorphosis.co/ep-37-miki-kashtan-on-the-three-shifts-needed-for-self-managing-organizations-to-thrive

to a more adult-adult dynamic (where individuals relate to each other as partners, collectively responsible for the organization's outcomes).

So how do we facilitate this shift, then? Of course, there's no one-size-fits-all solution here, but here are some starting points for facilitating the two human shifts Miki has outlined.

- **Upgrade our communication and relational skills:** For instance, try Nonviolent Communication training, or, for managers, training in how to be more empowering leaders.

- **Create spaces for "growth pain" conversations:** Frederic Laloux[2] recommends we create spaces for people to talk about the "growth pain" of letting go of our old identity and growing into a new one, whether it's through making coaches available or creating spaces (e.g., for middle managers) where growth pain can be spoken about, acknowledged, and transformed.

- **Build the capacity in teams to talk about what's "under the surface:"** In "power with," everyone is responsible for the working climate of their team (not the manager or HR), so it's vital to learn how to talk about what's "under the surface" (for instance, interpersonal dynamics, tensions, ways of being, etc.) and create agreements to design and maintain a working climate that's productive and inspiring to each member.

- **Embrace needs as an organizing principle:** Miki suggests that if we can dialogue about what the team or organization needs as well as what individuals need, it radically shifts the scope of possibility, for example when making decisions or designing roles.

I believe if we start taking steps toward these two human shifts, it will create a more robust platform on which to co-create new structures with new awareness.

---

2   You can watch the full video via Frederic Laloux's Insights for the Journey website here: https://thejourney.reinventingorganizations.com/4122.html

As organizational coach Simon Mont writes,[3]

"If you don't plan for the power relationships that you want, you will unconsciously reproduce the power relationships of the culture you inherited."

---

3   "Common mistakes in self-management" by Simon Mont https://medium.com/@ simon_83447/common-mistakes-in-self-management-introduction-2311001e8568

LISA GILL

Lisa Gill coaches teams and organizations who are interested in
becoming self-managing and facilitates leadership courses that train
people in a more adult coaching style
of leadership with Tuff Leadership
Training. She is also the host of the
Leadermorphosis podcast for which
she has interviewed thought leaders
and practitioners from all over the
world about the future of work. As
a writer she regularly contributes to
websites like Corporate Rebels as well
as her blog on Medium and was nominated for the EODF Best Written
Contribution Award. Lisa and some of her collaborators at Greater Than
have recently launched a facilitated online learning platform called Better
Work Together where people can practice and learn more about organizational self-management.

| LOCATION:
Barcelona, Spain

| EMAIL:
lisa@reimaginaire.com

| WEB SITES:
http://reimaginaire.com
http://tuffleadershiptraining.com
http://leadermorphosis.co
http://academy.betterworktogether.co

| SPECIALTIES:
- Self-managing teams and organizations
- Leadership training
- Liberating structures

| AVAILABLE FOR:
Coaching self-managing teams and organizations, conference speaking and workshop facilitation, leadership training, and online coaching and training.

ANDERSON

"You ever have one of those days where you just
don't feel like aligning?"

CREATING AGREEMENTS IS LIKE DISCOVERING SLICED BREAD

STEWART LEVINE

Organizations are known by their culture. That begs the question: What is the essence of an organization's culture, and is there a simple, elegant way of building and transforming this culture?

I wonder about this when I hear the phrase "cultural change" as the goal for a strategic initiative.

Regardless of how you might categorize or develop a particular culture, the ultimate key to satisfaction, success, accomplishment, and productivity is the ability to cultivate and sustain sequential and concurrent long-term relationships.

The quality of organizational relationships depends on the quality of the agreements among the people in the organization.

Unfortunately, most individuals have never developed the specific kind of conversational competence that enables them to create and maintain positive relationships.

Most of us never learned what to talk about when building agreements with team members, direct reports, supervisors, suppliers, and all other members of our virtual team. And we never learned how to deal with conflict in a non-adversarial way, or how to create ground rules for moving through challenging times.

I have come to call collaborative understandings between individuals "agreements for results."

Agreements impact every aspect of organizational life. You can create a culture of high trust relationships by elegantly crafting explicit agreements using the following conversational template.

Crafting "agreements for results" is a simple way of creating a culture that contains a high degree of trust because it's empowering, inclusive, and highly participatory.

THE TEN ELEMENTS OF AGREEMENTS FOR RESULTS

1 | **Intention and Specific Vision:** The big picture of what you intend to accomplish together must be specified. This provides a framework to hang the details on. A joint enterprise works best when everyone is working toward the same specific goals. The clearer the details of desired outcomes, the more likely you will attain them.

2 | **Roles and Necessary Parties:** The duties, responsibilities, and commitment of everyone must be clearly defined. Every person who's necessary for achieving the desired results must be part of the agreement.

3 | **Promises/Commitments to Action:** The agreement contains clear promises, so everyone knows who's responsible for what. When commitments to take action are specific, you can determine if the actions are sufficient to obtain the desired results and which actions *are missing.*

4 | Time and Value: All promises must have specific time deadlines for task completion. Value specifies who gets what for what. Is the exchange satisfactory? Does it provide adequate incentive?

5 | Measurements of Satisfaction: The evidence that everyone has achieved his or her objectives must be clear, direct, and measurable, so there can be no disagreement. Did you accomplish what you set out to do?

6 | Concerns and Fears: Bringing unspoken difficulties to the surface provides the opportunity to anticipate and minimize the disagreements that are bound to happen during collaboration.

7 | Renegotiation: No matter how optimistic and clear you are, it will become necessary to renegotiate promises and conditions of satisfaction. Circumstances change, and you must put in place a mechanism to address these new conditions.

8 | Consequences: Although you may not want to police the agreement, it's important to agree on consequences for anyone who breaks a promise.

9 | Conflict Resolution: Acknowledge that conflicts and disagreements arise as a matter of course when people work together. If you know that and establish an attitude of resolution and a process that leads to a new agreement, resolving conflicts will be easier.

10|Agreement? Trust (or lack thereof) is developed from the first nine aspects of this template. With these in play, everyone is satisfied and ready to take action. Work on the agreement until it is complete. Unless and until you are satisfied, do not move into action.

Have fun building a powerful culture using these agreements! It's like discovering sliced bread!

STEWART LEVINE

Stewart improves productivity while saving the enormous cost of conflict using "Agreements for Results" and "Resolutionary" conversational models. As a lawyer, he realized fighting is ineffective in resolving problems. At AT&T, he learned why collaborations fail: people do not create clarity about what they want to accomplish and how they will get there. He has worked across the organizational spectrum. His "Cycle of Resolution" is included in *The Change Handbook*.

His book *Resolution: Turning Conflict into Collaboration* was an Executive Book Club selection, featured by Executive Book Summaries, named one of the thirty best business books of 1998; and called "a marvelous book" by Dr. Stephen Covey. *The Book of Agreement* has been endorsed by many thought leaders, called "more practical" than the classic *Getting to Yes*, and named one of the best books of 2003. He co-authored *Collaborate 2.0*. He teaches communication, relationship management, and conflict management skills for The American Management Association, the University of California Berkeley Law School, and Dominican University Graduate Business School.

⊕ | LOCATION:

Alameda, a beautiful island in the Pacific off the coast of Oakland, California

✉ | EMAIL:

ResolutionWorks@msn.com

🖥 | WEB SITE:

https://ResolutionWorks.com

✏ | AUTHOR OF:

Resolution: Turning Conflict into Collaboration
The Book of Agreement
Collaborate 2.0 (co-author)

🏆 | SPECIALTIES:

- Resolving organizational conflict
- Coaching organizational leaders
- Creating cultures of agreement and resolution
- Teaching soft skills of all kinds
- Designing organizational or employee interventions

👤 | AVAILABLE FOR:

Coaching/mentoring, keynotes, training, and facilitation.

"Let's say your potential boss asks you to communicate with him exclusively via his hand puppet proxy, Mr. Handsington. How would you handle that?"

PERFORMANCE ISN'T ABOUT "PERFORMANCE" — IT'S ABOUT CONVERSATIONS

JOSH ALLAN DYSTRA

"Everybody is a genius. But if you judge a fish by its ability to climb a tree, it will live its whole life believing that it is stupid." —reportedly said by Albert Einstein

---

A lmost all approaches to "performance management" are pointless. Why?

In a nutshell, they make a fatally flawed assumption about people, which is the belief that *we can change our innate wiring.*

In other words, if I'm not "performing," there's something wrong with *me.* I'm inherently lacking *something*—knowledge, skills, effort, tenacity, and so forth—and if the organization could simply find a way to fill my deficit, whatever that is, I'd then magically "perform."

But this approach is the rough equivalent of spending hundreds of millions of dollars teaching fish to climb trees.[1] Of course, fish are physically incapable of doing this, so the entire nonsensical process just ends up frustrating you—and eventually killing the fish.

And that's what performance management often feels like, doesn't it?

In addition to this misunderstanding about the innate wiring of humans, we pile on top of it another mess of incorrect assumptions about feedback, which is an idea flawed almost to the point of uselessness.

Essentially, each of us have so much immovable cognitive bias that our feedback is always more about *us* than it is about the other person.[2] This means that when we share feedback, it's almost completely unhelpful as far as producing any kind of meaningful lift in performance.

Because my feedback mostly reflects *my* opinion about how to do something in a way that would be successful for *me* (not the recipient of the feedback), it just doesn't work. We're back trying to teach the trout to climb that oak in the yard.

HOW EXCELLENCE HAPPENS

The flawed notion of feedback leads directly into the next problem: our confusion about the nature of excellence itself. The popular label of performance management shows just how muddled we are, thinking that great performance could be somehow managed, controlled, and predicted like an equation.

---

1   *The Real Cost of Performance Reviews,* Reflective https://www.reflektive.com/blog/performance-review-cost/

2   *The Feedback Fallacy,* Harvard Business Review https://hbr.org/2019/03/the-feedback-fallacy

Truly brilliant performance is never managed—it's elicited, drawn out, liberated, coached, and nurtured. It's connected to what energizes us at fundamental levels. It coincides with states of flow, which seem to be most frequently expressed when we are working in service of a noble cause that feels magnetic.[3]

This means that what we call *performance* at work isn't really about performance at all, at least not in the heavy-handed, brute-force way it's handled today. In a great twist of irony, the way we approach performance is often one of the biggest obstacles to creating the level of performance we want to see.

So, if we can't achieve amazing performance through the current path, what do we do instead?

It's going to feel too simple (at first), so brace yourself.

We have *conversations.*

THE POWER OF DIALOGUE AND LANGUAGE

Yes, conversations. We double-down on recapturing the subtle art of dialogue and the near-infinite nuance of language and individual perspectives. We relearn how to be empathetic and look people in the eyes when they talk. We practice active listening, and we become competent in the art of shutting the hell up. (Hopefully now it feels sufficiently difficult for you.)

Enough trying to make tree-climbers of our finned friends—let's just put the fish in the water.

Let's stop pretending that the way great performance works for *me* has much of anything to do with the way it works for *you*, or that we could somehow make any of us better through stacking, ranking, numerical scales. Or through fear.

Let's build organizations that are about more than just making money, so people actually feel compelled to work toward something important.

And let's create work environments that allow each person to continually become the best, most energized version of themselves—and provide learning pathways to help them get there.

---

3   *How Work Can Heal the World*, TEDxYoungstown https://www.youtube.com/watch?v=ql_q0h4WGwE

We can do *so* much better than what we're doing now, and if we do, we'll see a lot more of that "great performance" we all want.

JOSH ALLAN DYKSTRA

Josh Allan Dykstra is a recognized thought leader on the future of work and company culture. He is an author, TEDx speaker, and the CEO of Helios, a community of leaders and work revolutionaries committed to creating a world where everyone can love work.

LOCATION:
Denver, Colorado

EMAIL:
hello@helios.work

WEB SITE:
https://helios.work

SPECIALTIES:
- The Energy-Based Operating System (ebOS) for work
- The future of work and "flatter" organizational structures
- Company culture as a primary business strategy
- A new approach to strengths/positive psychology at work

AVAILABLE FOR:
Keynote speaking, and C-level strategic advisory.

"I could go on and on about this. And I will.
Get comfortable."

THE CURE FOR DEATH BY POWERPOINT

RENÉE ANDRIANI

"Once the facts are clear, decisions jump out at you." —Peter Drucker

---

Think about the last time you attended one of your industry's conferences or corporate events. Sure, the food was good (and the open bar, if you were lucky), and it was fun catching up with people and sharing some laughs during breaks.

But most of the time you were probably in your seat, trying to give presenters your full attention, but fading fast and nearing information overload.

You wondered how tedious it was going to be to review all of the content with your boss or communicate everything effectively to your team. You questioned whether anything you said or contributed had resonated.

And if there had been just one more PowerPoint deck, your head may have exploded.

ENTER THE GRAPHIC RECORDER. WHAT'S A GRAPHIC RECORDER?

You may have seen a graphic recorder in action before. He or she would be working live at the meeting, usually off to the side of the podium or stage, writing and drawing on an enormous board with bold, colorful markers.

They listen to the speakers, distill the talking points, and convey them visually through words and pictures. Unlike static images in a PowerPoint, the content comes alive in real time.

This is particularly cool because the vast majority of us are visual learners. When we see ideas being clarified before us through pictures, we comprehend better and remember more. It promotes creativity and conversation with everyone in the room.

When our ideas and input are captured visually during workshops, break-out sessions, or discussions, we are validated and assured that our contributions are being shared.

Graphic recording maintains focus on the speaker's message and cultivates "same page" thinking as everyone sees the image evolve. People are less distracted, and the final artwork serves as the ideal tool to share with those who didn't attend.

Plus, it's *fun*. When people walk in to an event and see the markers and big white board, they know the stage is set for something interesting to happen. And at the conclusion, they see how their purpose and goals have been made tangible and concrete.

RENÉE ANDRIANI

Renée Andriani is a graphic recorder and illustrator. Her clients include Culture Ambassadors, Hilliard Lyons, University of Kansas Medical Center, Wells Fargo, Hallmark Cards, Scholastic, Terracon, Ascend Learning, and HarperCollins.

| LOCATION:
Kansas City, Missouri

| EMAIL:
randri4445@gmail.com

| WEB SITE:
https://randriani.carbonmade.com

| AVAILABLE FOR:
Graphic recording, event signage, and commissioned illustration and design.

© MARK ANDERSON, WWW.ANDERTOONS.COM

"OK, according to this there are three cars within a half mile. Which do you want to chase?"

STOP CHASING THE HAPPINESS GAP

JAMIE NOTTER

We call employee surveys many different things: employee engagement, employee experience, employee satisfaction, and so on. Yet in the end, nearly all of these surveys do exactly the same thing: they ascertain how happy people are. They all ask employees to weigh in on whether they like things the way they are right now. Do you like the feedback you're getting from your manager? Are you happy with your benefits package? Are we doing a good job on agility? Do you get to use your strengths at work? We seek positive responses to those questions, and if we get them, we pat ourselves on the back, and if we don't, we have now identified a problem to solve—a gap in happiness that we seek to fill.

The underlying premise of this process seems logical: if you find out where people are unhappy and then fix those pain points, you will make things better (improve engagement, retain top talent, create stronger teams, improve sales, etc.). There's just one problem: it doesn't work.

If you don't believe me, then how do you explain the fact that we have collectively been applying the "happiness gap" process described above to the issue of improving employee engagement for more than twenty years, yet we have barely increased the number of highly engaged employees (according to Gallup's numbers)? Seriously, we've spent literally billions of dollars between 2001 and 2018 only to see the "highly engaged" segment rise from 30 percent to a measly 34 percent. At that rate, we'll need another 297 years to get to 100 percent. Am I the only one who thinks these numbers prove that we're doing it wrong?

And here's *why* it doesn't work: the pain-point process only solves problems on the surface and ignores the underlying root causes. You're playing a game of whack-a-mole, constantly fixing one pain point based on this year's survey, only to find in next year's survey a different pain point to respond to. This will keep you very busy, but it won't move the needle on engagement or effectiveness because many of the pain points you fix turn out *not* to be the ones that are getting in the way of people being successful at work.

And that's the secret here. As much as we want to make our people happy, we'd be a lot better off helping them to be successful because being successful at work is the heart of engagement. So instead of asking them what they like, spend time finding out the underlying patterns inside your culture that are messing with success. If you fix those broken culture patterns, you'll start to see amazing results in terms of engagement and effectiveness.

For example, here's a culture pattern I see frequently in organizations related to innovation. Many organizations value innovation in their culture, but they tend to emphasize the concepts of innovation over the actions. Creativity and focusing on the future are emphasized and valued, but there isn't as much support for risk taking or experimentation. Typically, the only action-oriented building block of innovation I see supported in the culture is what we call "permission to hack." That is, if I want to change a process I'm working on, my manager will back me up.

So, here's the problem with that pattern. If "hacking" is your only outlet for innovation, your people will end up focusing their innovation efforts within their own work streams. You'll feel like there's a lot of innovation in the organization, yet all the individual efforts remain disconnected, and that means you're missing opportunities to connect the new developments early on—which is where you're more likely to derive much greater value from the innovation work. Bigger experiments or beta testing would solve that problem, but that's not valued in your culture, remember? If you asked your people if they liked how we are doing innovation, you'd probably get good scores, but until you find and fix the culture patterns that are getting in the way of unlocking the true potential of your innovation, you're missing out.

Stop asking your people about what they like and don't like, and spend your time and energy illuminating the subtle but important patterns inside your culture that are messing with success. When you start fixing the culture patterns (instead of the pain points), you'll finally start to see some of the results we've been missing over the last twenty years.

JAMIE NOTTER

Jamie Notter is an author and culture designer at Human Workplaces, where he helps leaders drive growth and engagement by aligning workplace culture with success. With twenty-five years of experience in conflict resolution, generational differences, and culture change, Jamie is also the co-author of three books—*Humanize*, *When Millennials Take Over*, and *The Non-Obvious Guide to Employee Engagement*—and holds a master's in conflict resolution from George

Mason and a certificate in Organization Development from Georgetown, where he also serves as adjunct faculty.

◉ | LOCATION:
Washington, DC

✉ | EMAIL:
jamie@humanworkplaces.net

🖥 | WEB SITE:
https://humanworkplaces.net

✎ | CO-AUTHOR OF:
Humanize
When Millennials Take Over
The Non-Obvious Guide to Employee Engagement

🏆 | SPECIALTIES:
- Culture design
- Culture management
- Generations and the impact of Millennials
- Conflict resolution

👤 | AVAILABLE FOR:
Culture assessments, culture consulting, and keynote speaking.

"How expensive would it be to just
skip practice and get right to perfect?"

VALUES ARE FOR LIVING
NOT LAMINATING

ALAN WILLIAMS

We are living in extraordinary times—volatile, uncertain, complex, ambiguous. The pace of change will never be this slow again. Many traditional approaches are no longer relevant and there is a new business agenda emerging. It has become fashionable for organizations to describe themselves as values-driven and yet, for the stakeholders (employees, customers, service partners, local communities, investors, members, citizens) of some, if not many, of these organizations, there is a disconnect between the organization's aspirational words and the stakeholders' experienced reality. Values are now mainstream; we have moved on from values just being a framed plaque on the wall. Values are now the organization's guiding compass and are most effective when they inform everything else an organization does.

*"In theory there is no difference between practice and theory.
In practice, there is." —Yogi Berra, baseball coach*

In keeping with Yogi Berra's quote, some leaders are great at the theory and talking about values but putting values into practice is an altogether different challenge, and far fewer leaders seem to be able to achieve this—in practice. Not many people believe that reading a coffee-table book about how to play tennis will enable them to play like Roger Federer or Serena Williams. So why do some leaders believe that articulating the values on a plaque on the wall or in a fancy presentation will make a values-driven organization? Why is it such a challenge to be a values-driven organization *in practice*? Here are four mistakes to avoid that organizations can make (and you might be able to add more to the list)? Consider how your own organization performs in each of these areas:

1 | **Lack of clarity.** "Clarity" means identifying the true values and clearly describing what they mean.

2 | **The values exist in theory rather than in practice.** "In practice" means putting the values into action throughout the organization.

3 | **Insufficient assessment.** "Assessment" means measuring the impact the values have internally and externally.

4 | **Lack of a development mind-set.** "Development" means learning from efforts and continuously developing the way the values are brought to life in everything that happens in the organization.

Which of these four areas do you think is the most important one to deal with? It's an unfair question because all four challenges need to be overcome all at the same time. If any one area is not addressed, then the organization will not be able to function in a truly values-driven way. The question asked earlier was "Why is it such a challenge to be a values-driven organization—in practice?" Perhaps you now have a better understanding of why this is the case.

And yet, none of these four challenges are impossible to overcome. Far from it. Improvement across the four areas does not involve a huge investment of time, money or other resources. What it does take, though, is a collective commitment led from the most senior level and throughout the whole organization, followed by a relentless determination to follow a values-driven path. Sustained success requires sustained effort, and leaders need to lead *in practice*. Think of the work we do in this area with progressive leaders of service organizations around the world as a pincer movement: actively guided from the boardroom, powered with passion from the frontline. This mind-set is supported with a set of tools to establish clarity, bring the values to life every day, measure stakeholder perception, and follow a robust process to maintain focus, discipline, and improvement. It's a tried and tested approach that delivers remarkable results (increased customer and employee attraction, retention, engagement and advocacy, increased sales and profit, more synergy, less waste and duplication). Values are for living not laminating.

Important note: Global Values Alliance[1] launched a Values Pledge in October 2019 to coincide with World Values Day.[2] The Values Pledge shows organizations how they can become values-driven. Signing the Values Pledge gives an important message to customers, employees, and other stakeholders that you are clear about what really matters to you and practice what you preach. If you are interested to know more about the Values Pledge, you can contact the Global Values Alliance at https://valuesalliance.net/join-us/ or Alan Williams at alan@servicebrandglobal.com.

---

1   https://valuesalliance.net/
2   http://www.worldvaluesday.com/

ALAN WILLIAMS

Alan Williams, Founder Director, SERVICEBRAND GLOBAL, coaches leaders of progressive service sector organizations, internationally and in the UK, to deliver values-driven service for sustained performance. He created the award-winning 31Practices approach to convert employees into brand ambassadors by translating organizational values into practical day-to-day behavior and is a published author and speaker whose projects have delivered measurable business impact across a balanced scorecard.

Alan is a past president of the UK Meetings Industry Association, a fellow of the Institute of Hospitality, a board member of BQF, a founding faculty Member of Culture University, a steering group member of the UK Values Alliance, and founder of the Global Values Alliance.

⊘ | LOCATION:

Global, wherever I need to be (otherwise London, UK)

✉ | EMAIL:

alan@servicebrandglobal.com

🖵 | WEB SITE:

http://servicebrandglobal.com

🏆 | SPECIALTIES:

- Designing, implementing and improving a SERVICEBRAND
- Values-driven service for sustained performance
- Brand identity
- Employee engagement
- Customer experience
- Values-driven leadership in practice and 31Practices
- The Values Economy

👤 | AVAILABLE FOR:

Coaching/mentoring, applying the SERVICEBRAND approach and associated Values Economy tools (including the award-winning 31Practices approach), keynote talks, and experiential working sessions.

"Neither one is better than the other, but if you want to be Team Celsius, that's fine."

EVERYONE VOLUNTARILY ENGAGES WITH THE MISSION

DOUG KIRKPATRICK

Every organization optimizes on something. W.L. Gore & Associates[1] is known as the most innovative company in America. To enjoy extraordinary customer service, customers can call Zappos[2] and chat with a cheerful representative for hours about shoes. Tomato giant Morning Star optimizes on simple core principles.

A principle[3] is a fundamental, primary, or general law or truth from which others are derived. Human principles are not unlike physical

---

1   https://www.gore.com
2   https://www.zappos.com
3   https://www.dictionary.com/browse/principle?s=t

principles (for example, gravity). Principles exist, and they're always working. People can choose to align their behavior with fundamental principles or not, but choosing to ignore principles (like gravity) can have serious consequences. On the other hand, aligning actions with principles conveys significant benefit.

SELF-MANAGEMENT IS FRACTAL MANAGEMENT

The world is becoming more complex. Human knowledge is doubling every twelve months.[4] The IBM study "Capitalizing on Complexity"[5] showed that most participating leaders felt overwhelmed by the complexity of business systems.

The path to managing complexity is, paradoxically, through simplicity. Simple principles allow for concentrated human effort. The fixed nature of principles allows people to exercise effective autonomy. The chain-of-command theory made sense when information moved one character at a time via Morse code. Today, chains of command forged in pursuit of the mirage of control are shackling organizational performance everywhere.

Self-managers connect with each other by voluntary agreement. When individual agreements are digitally rendered and relationally plotted, they resemble a spider web. A time-lapse video of such a diagram would change shape and size as individuals enter and leave the ecosystem. There is greater control, not less, when everyone is a manager.

A fractal[6] is a complex geometric pattern, exhibiting self-similarity in that details of structure at any scale repeat elements of the overall pattern. In a self-managed people network, core principles operate everywhere. One also finds management at every degree of magnification because in self-management, everyone is a manager. There is only work and people who work. This arrangement sustains enterprise agility—a critical success factor in a complex world.

---

4 http://www.industrytap.com/knowledge-doubling-every-12-months-soon-to-be-every-12-hours/3950
5 https://www.ibm.com/downloads/cas/1VZV5X8J
6 https://www.thefreedictionary.com/fractal

In a self-managed ecosystem, everyone voluntarily engages with the mission. The cultural DNA of respect for principle is embedded through language, education, modeling, and practice. This reinforcement reduces the risk of people acting contrary to the principles.

Since there are no barriers to communication anywhere in a network, fluid information catalyzes operational decision-making everywhere. A further powerful benefit of self-management is that innovation can and does arise from any point in the network.

Similarly, each peer in a self-managed organization has a voice in decisions that affect them. Self-management is not about voting or majority rule. It's about due process and protecting the voice of each member of the enterprise. Can peer-reviewed decisions take longer to make than those in a traditional structure? Absolutely. Is decision quality better with greater input? Definitely.

SELF-MANAGEMENT IS SCALABLE

According to a recent article in BBC Earth News,[7] scientists have recently discovered an ant mega-colony that has colonized much of the world, rivaling humans in the sheer scale of their global domination. The Argentine ant (Linepithema humile) mega-colony originated in South America but now spans much of the Mediterranean, California, and Western Japan— one super-colony apparently covers 6,000 kilometers of Mediterranean coastline. The ants' chemical hydrocarbon signatures provided proof of the common identity[8] of separate colonies existing on multiple continents.

These Argentine world travelers have a simple, two-pronged mission. First, they seek to survive; and second, to reproduce. Their mission is simple. As long as they focus on the mission, there are no barriers to scale.

Ants use chemical signals to coordinate. Self-managed professionals use information systems to provide feedback and coordinate activities, and adjust their "paths" accordingly. Ant colonies use division of labor to effectively feed themselves and modify their environments. Self-managed colleagues freely agree to act in concert with others or work individually.

---

7   http://news.bbc.co.uk/earth/hi/earth_news/newsid_8127000/8127519.stm
8   https://www.youtube.com/watch?v=rilDZP47N6Y

Individual ants take initiative in seeking food and shelter, chemically communicating promising trails to their fellow ants. Self-managed colleagues take initiative and create buy-in for their ideas and innovations. It's challenging to identify the leaders of an ant mega-colony—or of a self-managed organization. Leadership is fluid—and depends on the flow of commitments back and forth between the organization's members. If it's possible to grow without human bosses from zero to become the world's largest player in a global industry, then there are no inherent barriers to scale for a self-managed human enterprise.

Identifying sources of strategic competitive advantage is an existential challenge for any organization. Patents expire, trade secrets leak, talent walks, and technology is largely fungible. Superior methods of organizing and managing, however, represent an astronomical and largely untapped source of sustainable business advantage. In an age when information freely gushes everywhere, the future belongs to organizations that can engage every member with freedom, principle, and purpose.

DOUG KIRKPATRICK

Doug Kirkpatrick is an organizational change consultant, TEDx and keynote speaker, executive coach, author, and educator. He has been a regular contributor to the Huffington Post Blog on Great Work Cultures, and a partner in NuFocus Strategic Group, an international consulting firm where he leads organizational change, learning, and software initiatives to develop the networked, self-managed organizations of tomorrow.

He began his career in the manufacturing sector, principally with The Morning Star Company, a world leader in the food industry, as a financial controller. He now engages with Leadwise Community, People-Centric Organizations, Great Work Cultures, Work Revolution, Center for Innovative Cultures, Radical, and other vibrant organizations and leaders to co-create the future of management. The author of *Beyond Empowerment: The Age of the Self-Managed Organization* and co-author of *From Hierarchy to High Performance: Unleashing the Hidden Superpowers of Ordinary People to Realize Extraordinary Results*, Doug is launching a new title for Forbes Books, *The No-Limits Enterprise: Organizational Self-Management in the New World of Work*, released in 2019.

⊕ | LOCATION:
San Francisco, California

✉ | EMAIL:
d.kirkpatrick@nufocusgroup.com

🖵 | WEB SITES:
http://nufocusgroupusa.com
https://amzn.to/36FEyYt

🏆 | SPECIALTIES:
- Organizational innovation and self-management
- Creating the organization of the future
- Talent development
- The future of management
- The age of the self-managed organization
- The no-limits enterprise
- The new world of work

👤 | AVAILABLE FOR:
Organizational consulting, keynote speaking, leadership coaching, organizational assessments, Masterclasses, and curriculum design.

"When I grow up I either want to be a tastemaker or an influencer. But I'd settle for thought leader."

TIME'S UP

CLAUDETTE ROWLEY

We have the power, resources, knowledge, intellect, creativity, and heart to create a world based on parity, practical innovation, and potential. This is our planet—our global community—and it's time to transform our relationship to it and to each other.

When we save our planet, we save ourselves. That's the bottom line. We need a cultural revolution that allows us to look past political squabbles, lack of humanity, and what I call "reality resistance," or the unwillingness to examine empirical facts and data and observe the consequences of human behavior.

I believe that humanity is at a crossroads. Every day we hear stories of division, of disconnection from human kindness, and of people treating each other as though they don't matter. But we also hear stories of positive action, of strangers reaching out to help each other, and of joy, kindness, and celebration.

Every day we hear, read, and create both realities. The truth is this: we are all simply human beings. And when we drop the notion of differences between us, a new path of opportunity, choice, and connection emerges.

THE POWER OF BUSINESS TO INCITE CHANGE

The business world, through its influence on organizational culture, environmental resources, and government policy, is uniquely positioned to help us choose the path of human connection, dignity, and abundance.

This path doesn't sacrifice profitability, revenue generation, or innovation. In fact, most businesses haven't reached their full potential because they're out of alignment with their people, their culture, and their ability to anticipate and implement change.

What we know from quantum physics is that alignment matters. For example, the energy it takes to exploit your workforce to increase profits far outweighs the energy it would take to generate more revenue by respecting the people that work for you. When a business chooses to align its community impact with environmental needs, its products with human needs, and its corporate culture with employee needs, it becomes a force for good.

As more businesses choose to operate from the vantage point of self-awareness, respect, and kindness, the effect will be cumulative, changing the tenor of how we handle business globally. Your organization's ability to proactively respond to change is a key factor in your strategy, innovation, and conscious contribution to the world economy.

But we need the will. We need to realize that the *only* obstacle we face is the fear-based mindset of division we ourselves have created. We judge people, we hoard power, and we remain unconscious. In many corporations, people still think that respecting their workforce is optional and business success is just a numbers game. What will it take for us to wake up?

WE HAVE WHAT IT TAKES

If every nation on the globe worked together toward economic, social, and political parity, a new path would emerge. We can solve everything; we have all the resources we need. Why would we choose anything else? Yet every day, people, businesses, and governments opt for a different path.

This is an ultimatum. We require nothing less than a radical shift in cultural perspective. It's not about saving the earth; it's about providing humans a habitable place to live. This isn't about creating a society that's moral according to someone's religious definition; it's about harnessing the potential for creativity, innovation, and problem solving that resides in every human cell.

We're not talking about who's right or wrong; we need to realize that all of our actions stem from love or fear. And, every moment of every day, we get to choose. This is the ultimatum. And time's up. Choose wisely. So much more is possible than this.

CLAUDETTE ROWLEY

Claudette Rowley is the CEO of Cultural Brilliance, a cultural design and change management consultancy, and the author of *Cultural Brilliance: The DNA of Organizational Excellence* (2019). Over the past twenty years, Claudette Rowley has consulted at Fortune 1000 companies, small businesses, academic institutions, and start-ups, helping them create proactive and innovative workplace cultures that deliver outstanding results. She has served as the Chief Culture  Officer at Appli-Tec, a manufacturing company. Claudette is passionate about helping organizations resolve complex problems in ways that honor the intelligence of their cultural system and the brilliance of their people. She also hosts a globally syndicated radio show, *The Brilliance Ultimatum.* Claudette lives in the Greater Boston area.

⊕ | **LOCATION:**
Burlington, Massachusetts

✉ | **EMAIL:**
claudette@culturalbrilliance.com

💻 | **WEB SITE:**
https://culturalbrilliance.com

✏ | **AUTHOR OF:**
Cultural Brilliance: The DNA of Organizational Excellence
and
Embrace Your Brilliance: Align Yourself with Your Unique Potential

🏆 | **SPECIALTIES:**

- Designing and leading systemic cultural change
- Pre-change, pre-merger cultural assessment
- Leading large-scale change processes
- Leadership development programs
- Certified partner in the CultureTalk Survey System
- Executive coaching
- Strategic assessment and planning

👤 | **AVAILABLE FOR:**
Culture assessment, cultural design and implementation, executive coaching, leadership development, leading change, and strategic planning and design.

"We're taking a wait and see and then do
nothing approach."

WHY WAIT UNTIL SOMETHING GOES WRONG BEFORE DOING ANYTHING ABOUT ANYTHING?

DEREK MOWBRAY

In Europe, the cost of failing to prevent distress in the workplace amounts to about 650 billion Euros. We know that, in the UK, the average amount of time people spend away from their work healing their distress is about twenty-four days (which seems quite short but doesn't take account of the fact your life has changed and you never fully recover from stress). We know that people who experience distress also experience underperformance in that they lose their ability to concentrate, and concentration is fundamental to performance. Despite knowing all these brutal facts, nearly every type of workplace continues to turn a blind eye to the issues and prefers to wait until things go wrong before they do anything.

So, what is the problem? The problem is that most leaders in the workplace aren't leaders at all. They are people who manage processes. As I regularly say—processes need managers and management; people need leaders and leadership. The people who lead by following processes are comfortable with the technical aspects of life tend to like certainty. They don't like uncertainty and having to be so flexible and adaptive that they can interact effectively with people. Because most leaders don't like this uncertainty, they don't lead. If they don't lead, there is no one looking after the psychological interests of the workforce. Hence the massive amounts of money lost to psychopresenteeism—people coming to work in body but not in mind.

If the problem is that the workplace has no leaders, a follow-up problem is that people are scared to speak about the main problem. The workforce doesn't say "My manager doesn't have a clue how to lead" for fear of someone attacking their self-esteem by sacking them. So, the culture of fear dominates in the workplace; and the result is that most organizations fail to realize their true and full potential.

Working in a client organization recently, I started out by saying much of what I've written above. The Chief Executive responded by telling me his organization was a great success. This prompted me to ask why I was invited to talk to him and his board if everything was going brilliantly. The CEO didn't know why I had been invited; but the human resources specialist knew—it was because the staff attrition rate was 25 percent. So, while the CEO thought the return to shareholders, and level of profit, made the organization a huge success, the attrition rate indicates a fundamentally poorly functioning outfit. So, I told the CEO he was nowhere near being as successful as he could be.

I also told him by following The Wellbeing and Performance Agenda, a systemic approach to creating and sustaining a psychologically healthy and safe organization, he would be able to achieve greater success than he could possibly imagine. It would mean he'd have to train as a BOLD and Adaptive Leader, along with everyone else in the organization, but that it would all be worthwhile as his business would become a place that buzzed with excitement, humor, joy, and hard work.

He declined. He wants to wait until things go wrong before doing anything about anything.

DEREK MOWBRAY

Derek Mowbray is an organization health psychologist and behavior scientist with a special interest in the prevention of stress in the workplace. He specializes in leadership development and the application of The Wellbeing and Performance Agenda to all forms of organization. His initiative in developing psychological responsibility and sharing responsibility for the success of the organization has changed the way many organizations function in the UK and around the world.

Derek Mowbray recently relinquished his role as visiting professor of psychology at two UK universities, but he continues in his role as independent technical expert for psychological wellbeing to the European Commission, as well as being director of several businesses, all geared to preventing stress and provoking psychological wellbeing at work.

🌐 | LOCATION:
Gloucestershire, UK

✉ | EMAIL:
derek.mowbray@mas.org.uk

🖥 | WEB SITE:
http://mas.org.uk

✏ | AUTHOR OF:
Guides to All Aspects of The Well-Being and Performance Agenda
and
eLearning programs in Personal Resilience and The Manager's Role in Resilience

🏆 | SPECIALTIES:
- Facilitating the implementation of The Wellbeing and Performance Agenda
- BOLD and Adaptive Leadership development
- Resilience at organization, team, and individual levels
- Resolution of extreme conflicts

👤 | AVAILABLE FOR:
Facilitating change in organizations, facilitating workshops, keynote speaking, consultancy, and conflict resolution.

"Enough with the pleasantries..."

LOVE: IT CHANGES EVERYTHING

GAYLE VAN GILS

Why am I bringing up the "l" word in a business book? In the words of Tina Turner: "What's love got to do with it?"

The answer is—everything.

Love is an expansive emotion. It opens us up. It helps connect us to what we are doing and to each other. It is also the emotion that makes us vulnerable and available. Unfortunately, that can feel dangerous in many business cultures.

Let me share a story.

Years ago, I worked in a huge aerospace company on the west coast. It was a culture that had rules for everything and demanded strict compliance. In my role, I was tasked with creating training for new hires that would indoctrinate them into the culture and make sure they adapted.

Frankly it was a culture that did not trust people, a company ruled by fear—the very opposite of love. Because no one felt safe there, the atmosphere shut down innovative thinking, genuine connection, and the sharing of ideas and resources. The best people left, and turnover was high. The words "I don't feel safe to express that," or "I don't feel safe to do that," came up often.

During the same time I was working there and in all the years since, I have been conducting trainings using the practice of mindfulness to help develop self-awareness, self-love, and compassion. This training is designed to allow individuals to get in touch with their own goodness.

At the end of a weekend training, I often hear the same, often tearfully delivered comment, "I feel so good and open and feeling like this, I don't feel safe to go to work tomorrow. I'll be crushed!" I began to realize that the pervasive fear in the workplace was a cultural issue that needed to be addressed directly with many of the same tools that I was already using.

OPENING OUR HEARTS = OPENING OUR MINDS

Goodness in life is connected with opening our hearts and tearing down the walls that separate us from each other and keep us from being intimately in touch with our world. It takes a lot of courage to open our hearts to ourselves in the workplace—a place that may not feel safe due to current norms of behavior. Yet doing so is exactly the answer to the constriction that cuts off communication and collaboration in an unhealthy work environment.

When you open yourself to feel, you also open the door for others to feel and communicate with you.

When your behavior is inspired by love and connection versus the fear and constriction that often dominates at work, your mind becomes more curious, creative, collaborative, and compassionate. An open mind is interested and has the patience to listen and consider other points of view.

When our minds open to truly take in more than our own position and desires, we make it possible to shift the culture of our workplaces away from narrow and egotistical orientations. When we no longer feel shut down or afraid to share our talents, we reap an outpouring of ideas and innovation.

THE FUTURE IS FLEXIBLE

Today's workplaces can only thrive if we discover and implement strategies that reduce and manage stress and encourage flexible thinking and open communication. This will allow our businesses to prosper in these times of uncertainty, global competition, resource depletion, and an ever-growing knowledge economy.

Companies such as Aetna, Goldman Sachs, Black Rock, General Mills, Green Mountain Coffee, SAP, and others have implemented mindfulness programs. As a result, they're experiencing a happier and healthier workforce that is more focused, less stressed, and more productive.

The ways in which mindfulness and love as compassionate engagement can work to improve our lives and livelihood is the next frontier in business practice. Love is the emotion that opens our hears and connects us to each other and to the greater good, and it's what is needed to cure the dysfunctions of the modern workplace.

GAYLE VAN GILS

Gayle Van Gils is the award-winning author of *Happier at Work: The Power of Love to Transform the Workplace,* a practical guide for developing the powers of attention, stress reduction, communication, and collaboration. She is a certified instructor of Search Inside Yourself,[1] the mindfulness and emotional intelligence training developed and proven at Google, and a senior meditation teacher in the Shambhala Buddhist lineage.

Gayle is the founder of the consulting, training, and coaching company Transform Your Culture,[2] where she utilizes her certification as a Barrett Values Center Consultant[3] to help you align personal and company values with success. Gayle is also a mindfulness teacher on the app Simple Habit,[4] where thousands enjoy her diverse meditations. Through her teachings, both in person and through online courses, Gayle helps individuals to find more peace, energy, inspiration, joy, and success in their lives and businesses.

---

1 https://siyli.org
2 https://transformyourculture.com
3 https://www.valuescentre.com
4 https://blog.simplehabit.com/2017/05/25/mindfulness-at-work-with-gayle-van-gils/

◉ | LOCATION:

St. Petersburg, Florida

✉ | EMAIL:

gayle@transformyourculture.com

🖵 | WEB SITES:

https://transformyourculture.com/

https://amazon.com/dp/B072HTB246

https://siyli.org/

https://valuescentre.com/

https://bit.ly/35uIDgy

✎ | AUTHOR OF:

Happier at Work: The Power of Love to Transform the Workplace

🏆 | SPECIALTIES:

- Strategic culture transformation
- The ENGAGE System for Workplace Engagement, Happiness and Productivity
- Mindfulness and emotional intelligence training
- Leadership mentoring
- Barrett Cultural Values Surveys certified consultant
- Search Inside Yourself certified teacher (developed at Google)

👤 | AVAILABLE FOR:

Culture assessments, culture consulting, keynote speaking, executive coaching, mindfulness training, emotional intelligence training, strategic planning.

"It's a brand new position, and we're still figuring out your duties. So I won't be able to tell you how you're doing it wrong for a few weeks."

WHY YOU SHOULD CARE ABOUT HOW WORK GETS DONE -- AND NOT JUST WHAT'S ACCOMPLISHED

JOSH LEVINE

Maybe once upon a time, companies didn't care how employees hit their numbers. If it wasn't illegal, it was fair game—an admittedly low bar that many still fail to reach.

But these days, customer reviews and social media foster a higher level of accountability.

Some brands have even taken to advertising their "hows." Lyft's It Matters How You Get There,[1] and Bank of the West's Change Matters[2] are two recent examples.

---

1 https://vimeo.com/237319655
2 https://changematters.bankofthewest.com/change/

For decades, "Sell more, and you'll be rich" was the charge. Today's version might be "ship faster" or "capture clicks," but the message to the employee is the same: do what it takes.

But solely rewarding behaviors that drive short-term corporate wins over long-term customer benefits can cause severe damage to a company's reputation.

TRADING LONG-TERM SUCCESS FOR SHORT-TERM CASH

Alex, (not his real name), is a territory sales manager for a medical device company. Like any sales group, he and his team know their paychecks depend on hitting those numbers.

Alex has been in this industry for over ten years, and he understands that this month's sales come from work he put in six to twelve months ago. His success relies on relationships, and his job is building trust among all the individuals he encounters. When product sales and trust-building align, all is well, but what happens when they are at odds?

Alex explains that not every device or supply he sells is going to serve the patient the best. "I have to make a choice: do I move a product that I don't believe is the best solution for the patient, or recommend a better one from another brand?" The conflict between trust and sales can intensify further when his company publishes its annual list of "must sell" items, a subset of about twenty-five product lines from their catalog of over one hundred.

Luckily for the company, the surgeon, and the patient, Alex is uncompromising. "[The company] is asking me to trade long-term success for short-term sales. I'm just not going to do that."

Others may not be as clear-headed. Whether advocating for an inferior product or opening fake accounts, sales professionals play the game to win.

But could Alex's organization reward relationships, in addition to sales numbers, in order to strengthen short- and long-term success? It wouldn't be as easy to track, but it is possible.

RECOGNIZING THE HOW

There are a few examples out there of companies that prioritize more than just outcomes.

Perhaps one of the oldest examples is Disney's "The Spirit of FRED Award." Fred was an early employee of Disney who transitioned from hourly to full-time. It was during his time that a few would-be mentors shared the critical characteristics of the people who worked at the house the mouse built. Coincidentally, those characteristics are: Friendly, Resourceful, Enthusiastic, and Dependable—or FRED. Whether or not this origin story is accurate, Disney continues to hand out this award, recognizing people who embody the spirit of FRED.

A more contemporary and scalable example comes from PagerDuty, a San Francisco–based software company that recently went public.[3] Employees and managers at PageDuty recognize one another for actions that align with the company's values.

Anyone can post a shout-out tagged with the associated value through Slack, or performance review software Reflektive. The post appears on screens mounted throughout their offices in all locations. The supportive statements also show up in a weekly email digest.

What's more, each post gets tracked and tallied for employee reviews. Managers can see which values an employee has racked up in the past six months and where they might be lacking. This accounting of employee decision-making becomes the hard data that guides feedback.

WHAT'S MEASURED IS WHAT MATTERS

There are many ways to climb a mountain. Setting a goal to reach the summit can inspire, but the destination alone won't tell you which trail to take. Unfortunately, that's what happens too often in business. When only rewarding results, even the most talented may choose the wrong route—shortcuts that undermine broader business objectives. In a well-designed culture, the end should never justify the means.

---

3   https://medium.com/great-monday/what-makes-a-culture-ipo-ready-4d72e3923e8c

Every business outcome is the effect of how people work. The best way to achieve any goal consistently (and honestly) is recognizing behaviors that lead to those ends, not merely the results themselves.

Attempting to shortcut the cycle leads to dangerous choices and dysfunctional cultures. Incentivizing employees to influence the outcome directly is like paying babysitters for how much food they get your kids to eat. It might be effective at first, but eventually, how they do the rest of their job suffers.

If leaders are going to change how they manage organizations, they must recognize and reward values-driven choices as well as outcomes. Pointing out an individual or team will make employees proud of what they did and continue that behavior. What's more, this approach amplifies the positive effect; when others see positive recognition, they'll emulate that behavior, too.

If we care about how the work gets done, not only what gets accomplished, we need to change how we measure and reward work. After all, what gets measured gets managed, and what gets managed matters. Rewarding values-driven behaviors is how the best leaders of the future get the best results from the best people.

JOSH LEVINE

Josh Levine is a best-selling author, brand strategist, and a highly sought-after speaker on a mission to help organizations design a culture advantage. For more than fifteen years, Levine has helped build culture-driven brands for a wide range of organizations—including Silicon Valley heavy hitters, prominent nonprofits, and well-respected blue-chip corporations. He is best known as the co-founder of the nonprofit CULTURE LABx and, as an executive director, helped it flourish into an international community. His new book, *Great Mondays*, which was recently listed on BookAuthority's list of the best culture books of all time, teaches organizations how to design a company culture employees love.

Levine is recognized for his entertaining, energetic, and educational keynotes that reveal fresh insights and inspire new action. He teaches brand strategy and culture design courses in the groundbreaking MBA program of Design at the California College of the Arts to motivate the next generation of leaders. Levine is a columnist at Forbes.com, and his work has been featured in Huffington Post, *Fast Company*, and the *Design Management Journal*. He holds a BS in Engineering Psychology from Tufts University and BFA in design from the Academy of Art University.

⊕ | LOCATION:
San Francisco, California

✉ | EMAIL:
josh@greatmondays.com

🖵 | WEB SITE:
https://greatmondays.com

🏆 | SPECIALTIES:
- Culture audit
- Values development
- Employer value proposition
- Talent campaign strategy
- Employer branding
- Talent recognition programs
- Culture activation platform

👤 | AVAILABLE FOR:
Consulting, executive, and team workshops and keynotes.

"I find it helps if you think of it as less of a messy desk and more of an archeological dig."

WHAT SORT OF CULTURE ARE WE TALKING ABOUT, EXACTLY?

JENNIFER HANCOCK

Everyone has an operating philosophy, or a set of ideas that drives their thinking and behavior. Everyone also has their own set of values.

The problem is, we often don't see evidence of those values in the workplace. Not all corporate cultures are positive. Some are downright toxic.

Strategy consultant Adam Cox once told me that corporate culture is defined by the last person who was promoted, and he's right. When you promote a cutthroat or mean person, you create a cutthroat culture.

Businesses and managers focused on bottom-line economic success rarely consider the ethical implications of their decisions on their workers or the business itself. And they rarely consider the impact their decisions are having on corporate culture.

I'm guessing every cultural ambassador would like to change that!

The question is, what should we change it to? What exactly are the cultural values we want to promote?

WHAT DOES CULTURAL CHANGE LOOK LIKE?

Most likely, we all want our workplaces to be happier and nicer—more humanistic. But what does that mean exactly? What are the values we should be promoting to create that?

I personally have three required conditions for happy and humanistic workplaces.

I feel happy at work when:

1 | I am treated with dignity.

2 | The work that I do matters.

3 | Problem-solving is fun, not frustrating, meaning we solve problems collaboratively and in the best interest of our customers.

Treating everyone with dignity and worth makes everyone feel respected. It's a good cultural value to aim for. It's measurable, and it also means that bullies or mean-spirited people are incompatible with a good workplace culture. We need to encourage and promote the giving, getting, and being of dignity.

Making sure the work you are doing matters is also important. It gives our lives meaning and purpose and helps us feel motivated. Even if you are asking someone to sweep the floor, that task matters.

The best way to figure out why work matters is to consider what happens if the work isn't done. If nothing bad happens when the work isn't done, maybe the work doesn't matter, and you should direct your staff to work that does.

Knowing why the work matters helps employees understand why it's important to get the work done right. This brings me to the third point: good, effective, and ethical problem solving.

All businesses are in the business of solving problems. If they aren't solving problems, they aren't in business long. How we solve problems matters, and it defines what our corporate culture is like. Ideally, we should be problem solving in an effective, ethical, and collaborative way.

What usually happens is that problem solving in the workplace is done through bullying and competition. Who's the loudest? Who can control the conversation? Who denigrates the ideas of others? Or worse, we deal with bullies who exclude people from the problem-solving process altogether.

I have never talked to a manager who hired someone to not work. And yet, many managers allow bullies to exclude people from the work process. We should not allow that to happen. We need to treat each contributor as equal and not allow bullies to exclude anyone because, ideally, everyone should be collaborating to solve our problems ethically and effectively.

To change the culture around problem solving so that it is truly collaborative and humanistic, we need to prioritize and continually reinforce our goal, which is to collaborate so that we can effectively and ethically solve our problems.

If we do not prioritize and reward collaborative and ethical problem solving, it will never be part of our corporate cultures. If we do not prioritize the giving and getting of dignity for every person in the workplace so that everyone can be part of the collaboration, it will never be part of our corporate culture, either.

LEADING BY EXAMPLE

Happy, ethical, and humanistic workplaces filled with dignity and compassion are what we should aspire to as individuals and leaders. It should exemplify how we treat our colleagues. We should be modeling ethically responsible and collaborative problem solving, and we should be expecting the same from every one of our colleagues.

It's not enough for cultural ambassadors to talk about culture; we should be specific about exactly what sort of culture we want to have.

Personally, I want happy humanistic workplaces.

How about you?

JENNIFER HANCOCK

Jennifer Hancock is the founder of Humanist Learning Systems. She is a mom, author of several books, and founder of Humanist Learning Systems. Jennifer is considered one of the top speakers and writers in the world of humanism today. Her professional background is varied, including stints in both the for-profit and non-profit sectors. She served as Director of Volunteer Services for the Los Angeles SPCA, sold international franchise licenses for a biotech firm, was the Manager of Acquisition Group Information for a half-billion-dollar company, and served as the executive director for the Humanists of Florida. Shortly after her son was born, she published her first book, *The Humanist Approach to Happiness: Practical Wisdom*. Her speaking and teaching business coalesced into the founding of Humanist Learning Systems that provides online personal and professional development training in humanistic business management and science-based harassment training that actually works.

Jennifer's new book (2019) is *Applied Humanism: How To Create More Effective And Ethical Businesses*[1].

---

1   https://bit.ly/2uqoStJ

◉ | LOCATION:

Florida

✉ | EMAIL:

jenhancock@humanistlearning.info

🖥 | WEB SITE:

https://humanistlearning.com

✎ | AUTHOR OF:

The Humanist Approach to Happiness: Practical Wisdom
and
Applied Humanism: How To Create More Effective And Ethical Businesses

🏆 | SPECIALTIES:

- Ending harassment using behavioral psychology
- Humanistic management
- Change management using behavioral psychology
- Integrating ethics into strategic planning

👤 | AVAILABLE FOR:

Online and in-person training, EEO and sexual harassment training, radio and TV interviews, and public speaking.

"You know, destruction aside, he really lives up to the hype."

HELPING US TO SMILE AND LAUGH

MARK ANDERSON
ESSAYS FROM THE EDGE CARTOONIST

From an early age, I loved to draw and tell jokes.

I tried to persuade my teachers to let me do my homework as cartoons. When they said no, I drew in the margins. I took a cartooning class at a local library and got to rub shoulders with a working cartoonist. When my high school art teacher saw my cartoons, he told me to go to the school newspaper office and introduce myself as the new cartoonist and I did just that.

I drew for the high school and college newspapers and graduated from the University of Northern Iowa with a music degree. I moved to Chicago, married my college sweetheart, and found a job in a screw factory.

Bored, I would draw cartoons at the coffee table in my spare time. I submitted my work to magazines, and to my surprise, they started buying.

I kept writing and drawing cartoons early in the morning, on lunch hour, and late at night. When my first child was born, I quit my job to be a stay-at-home dad and draw cartoons full-time.

I have the best job in the world—professional cartoonist, running andertoons.com, and teaching cartooning at schools and libraries.

I am a member of the National Cartoonists Society and have been a featured speaker at their annual Reuben Awards. I have also spoken at the Kenosha Festival of Cartooning, taught at two Success in Comics seminars, and written for the International Journal of Comic Art. I also have a cartoon displayed in the Smithsonian Museum of American History and am syndicated online by Universal.

| LOCATION:
Chicago, Illinois

| EMAIL:
mark@andertoons.com

| WEB SITE:
http://andertoons.com

| SPECIALTIES:
- Cartoons
- Humorous illustrations

| AVAILABLE FOR:
Social media, emails, blogs, and anything else that needs a funny touch.

"Hey everyone, the answer is love! You can start climbing back down now!"

KIND, CONSCIOUS COMMUNICATOR

HANNAH SENTENAC
ESSAYS FROM THE EDGE EDITOR

A master of all things media, I'm a writer, editor, and content creator who's passionate about helping people and products shine their brightest.

A pop culture expert and enthusiast, I do my best to live a kind, conscious, and cruelty-free life—all while having as much fun as possible! My mission is to show people that we can

have all the things we love and enjoy without doing harm to the planet, people, or our animal friends.

Jerry found me several years ago, and I've loved working with him to showcase the crucially important topic of workplace wellbeing—because we all deserve to be happy at work and at home!

Travel, fashion, food, drinks, mental health, and general wellness are my areas of expertise, and I share this passion with the world via all kinds of content creation. I work with brands, individuals, and media outlets that share my vision of a kind, joyful, and loving way of life.

I'm trained in journalism, and I've worked for major news outlets across the country. I've interviewed celebs, written viral gems, launched popular blogs, and spun creative tales for clients and publications large and small.

I'm always looking to connect with other like-minded folks, so please feel free to reach out and say hi anytime!

⊕ | LOCATION:
Los Angeles, California

✉ | EMAIL:
hannah.sentenac@gmail.com

🖵 | WEB SITES:
http://hannahsentenac.com
http://somevegangirl.com

🏆 | SPECIALTIES:
- Content creation
- Communications strategy
- Plant-based and conscious food/travel/lifestyle consulting

👤 | AVAILABLE FOR:
Copywriting, content planning/creation, lifestyle/ trend consulting, editing, public speaking, and hosting.